NEW DIRECTIONS FOR PHILANTHROPIC FUNDRAISING

Cathlene Williams
Association of Fundraising Professionals

Lilya Wagner
The Center on Philanthropy at Indiana University

COEDITORS-IN-CHIEF

EXPLORING BLACK PHILANTHROPY

Patrick Rooney
The Center on Philanthropy at Indiana University

Lois Sherman
The Center on Philanthropy at Indiana University

EDITORS

T0340146

Numbe

Summe

JOSSEY-BASS™
An Imprint of
WILEY

EXPLORING BLACK PHILANTHROPY
Patrick Rooney, Lois Sherman (eds.)
New Directions for Philanthropic Fundraising, No. 48, Summer 2005
Cathlene Williams, Lilya Wagner, Coeditors-in-Chief

NEW DIRECTIONS FOR PHILANTHROPIC FUNDRAISING (print ISSN 1072-172X; online
ISSN 1542-7846) is indexed in Higher Education Abstracts and Philanthropic Index.

Microfilm copies of issues and articles are available in 16 mm and 35 mm, as well as
microfiche in 105 mm, through University Microfilms Inc., 300 North Zeeb Road,
Ann Arbor, Michigan 48106-1346.

NEW DIRECTIONS FOR PHILANTHROPIC FUNDRAISING is part of the Jossey-Bass
Nonprofit and Public Management Series and is published quarterly by Wiley
Subscription Services, Inc., A Wiley company, at Jossey-Bass, 989 Market Street,
San Francisco, California 94103-1741.

SUBSCRIPTIONS cost $109.00 for individuals and $215.00 for institutions, agencies,
and libraries. Prices subject to change. Refer to the order form at the back of this
issue.

EDITORIAL CORRESPONDENCE should be sent to Lilya Wagner, The Center on Philanthropy at Indiana University, 550 West North Street, Suite 301, Indianapolis, IN
46202-3162, or to Cathlene Williams, Association of Fundraising Professionals,
1101 King Street, Suite 700, Alexandria, VA 22314.

www.josseybass.com

Contents

Editors' Notes

THIS ISSUE OF *New Directions for Philanthropic Fundraising* is based on the Seventeenth Annual Symposium on Philanthropy held in Indianapolis on August 26–27, 2004. Scholars, donors, fundraisers, and other practitioners came together to discuss and reflect on current and historical issues surrounding black philanthropy. The chapter authors address the theoretical, practical, and applied factors supporting and confronting black philanthropy.

Emmett Carson leads this issue with a provocative delineation of the past, present, and future of black philanthropy. In Chapter One, he challenges us to consider what black philanthropy has meant and how we will react when it changes as black culture, society, and values change. He points out that black leaders may not be happy about all of the changes. For example, as more black families join the middle and upper socioeconomic groups, their philanthropy may shift from nonprofits focused on black issues and black religious groups to a more comprehensive set of nonprofits.

Charles Stephens was invited to give the annual lecture honoring the career of Arthur C. Frantzreb and addressed professionalism in black philanthropy. In Chapter Two, he delineates three C's required to achieve full professional status: a common curriculum, a common code of ethics, and a comprehensively accepted certification. While he points out that the profession as a whole is making great progress toward meeting these criteria, he challenges us on the role of the black professional in this mix, noting that minorities constitute less than 10 percent of membership in the Association of Fundraising Professionals and only 3 percent of the Council for Advancement and Support of Education. Less than 1 percent of fundraising professional certifications are held by blacks.

NEW DIRECTIONS FOR PHILANTHROPIC FUNDRAISING, NO. 48, SUMMER 2005 © WILEY PERIODICALS, INC.

Combining results from a survey, a set of interviews, and Web searches of black megachurches (those with more than twenty-five hundred members), Cheryl Hall-Russell finds several important recurring trends that shape their philanthropy. She notes in Chapter Three that most of the members are middle class. There has been an emphasis on bringing males back into the church and supporting black businesses. A majority of the churches have their own K–8 schools. Most had community development corporations and were major employers in their communities.

Felinda Mottino and Eugene Miller report in Chapter Four on African American donors in the New York metropolitan region. They interviewed 166 minority donors in the region, including 58 African American donors. They review the attitudes and motivations about philanthropy in these groups with a special focus on pre– and post–civil rights legislation. They report conspicuous differences in giving levels and communities of interest between the pre–and post–Civil rights era donors.

John Havens and Paul Schervish extend their wealth transfer model to African American households in Chapter Five. They find that in 2001, African Americans constituted 12.4 percent of all households in the United States, earned 7.1 percent of total personal income, and owned 2.5 percent of net worth, while contributing 5.4 percent of total household giving.

Richard Steinberg and Mark Wilhelm review in Chapter Six differences in religious and secular giving by race and ethnicity using the Center on Philanthropy Panel Study (COPPS). This is the largest data set ($N = 7,400$) that has ever asked about philanthropy in the United States. They use this very rich data set to look for differences in both the average levels of giving by race and ethnicity but also after controlling for differences in income and education.

In Chapter Seven, Sheila Suess Kennedy revisits some of the issues surrounding church and state and the Charitable Choice provisions of the 1996 welfare reform law. This law permitted legal discrimination in hiring to preserve the religious nature of the organization. She points out that some of these provisions were attacked from both the political left and right. Others expressed concerns about regulatory burdens. Kennedy also discusses the three C's of charitable choice: capacity, commitment, and constitutionality.

In Chapter Eight, Jacqueline Copeland-Carson outlines trends in black philanthropy that stem from the African diaspora. She proposes a more expansive notion of black philanthropy to include diverse practices of native-born black Americans as well as those of contemporary immigrants to the United States from Africa, the Caribbean, and Latin America. She regrets the paucity of studies of either African or black philanthropy in a diasporan context and offers her observations as suggestive of areas for future research, not as definitive conclusions or prescriptions for action.

Una Okonkwo Osili and Dan Du, also using COPPS data, ask whether the philanthropic behaviors of immigrants differ from those of native-born Americans. Using this large national data set, they find no significant difference in either the incidence or levels of giving between immigrants and all others. However, immigrants are significantly more likely to transfer funds to their friends and families from home.

John Stanfield delineates a personal biography of becoming a researcher of race philanthropy and appeals for research to outline policy strategies and civic participation practices for a multiracial society. Chapter Ten is situated in the context of the evolution of African American studies and the role of sociology in these studies in the postwar era.

Alice Green Burnette delivered the annual Donikian Family Lecture at the symposium, "Hopscotching in the Neighborhood." This playfully serious analysis, completing this issue in Chapter Eleven, discusses the nine steps to raising money in the black community. These range from understanding the technical aspects of fundraising and the socioeconomic demographics of one's donors to more qualitative issues like understanding the depth and texture of relationship building in the black community.

This special issue of *New Directions* focuses on varied aspects of black philanthropy, an important topic to our philanthropic society both today and in the future. We have viewed this topic through several lenses: practice, history, economics, sociology, and constitutional law. Each of these brings different aspects of black philanthropy into focus. It is our hope that collectively, we have provided a comprehensive and interesting combination of chapters that help illuminate these issues.

Patrick Rooney
Lois Sherman
Editors

PATRICK ROONEY *is director of research at the Center on Philanthropy at Indiana University.*

LOIS SHERMAN *is publications and Web site manager at the Center on Philanthropy at Indiana University.*

A brief look at the past and present helps inform speculation about the future of black philanthropy and how it may affect America's nonprofit sector.

1

Black philanthropy's past, present, and future

Emmett D. Carson

IN THE PAST TEN years, black philanthropy has moved from relative obscurity to become the focus of national and regional conferences as well as a growing area of study by scholars. This is a welcome change brought about by the growing recognition that African Americans have a rich philanthropic tradition and that the changing demographics of American society coupled with greater socioeconomic equality will result in African American philanthropy's playing an ever greater role in shaping the direction and contours of the American nonprofit sector.

This chapter explores black philanthropy's proud past and the socioeconomic forces that helped to shape it, examines black philanthropy today and how it differs from the past, and speculates about the future of black philanthropy and its impact on nonprofit organizations interested in soliciting gifts from African Americans.

It is important to provide some context at the start for the issues expressed in this chapter, as well as two critical definitions. It is increasingly difficult to have segregated conversations within a racial or ethnic group that are not overheard and possibly taken out of context by other racial and ethnic groups. For example, comments

NEW DIRECTIONS FOR PHILANTHROPIC FUNDRAISING, NO. 48, SUMMER 2005 © WILEY PERIODICALS, INC.

by entertainer Bill Cosby that some African American parents are too young and are not adequately fulfilling their parental responsibilities caused a national stir. Cosby's comments, in a May 2004 speech, were directed to an African American audience and were widely taken out of context by both right-wing conservatives and advocates of the African American community. The ideas put forward in this chapter are meant to provoke a candid discussion about the current state and future of black philanthropy by those who want to promote knowledge and open discussion and not whether they are the right or wrong choices for the African American community.

While black philanthropy is often discussed, few provide a working definition. Black philanthropy is defined here to mean the giving of time, talent, goods, and services or money by African Americans for charitable purposes. Black philanthropy should not be viewed as limited to charitable donations by African Americans to African American causes or organizations, as some believe. After all, white philanthropy has never been defined by the recipient of the charity or the charitable gift. Is a gift no less black philanthropy when it comes from African American hands but supports such institutions as Harvard University?

The second concept to convey is that black philanthropy is not a static concept but rather an evolving, fluid concept that adapts based on its environment. Carson's axiom, modestly named, is that black philanthropy is shaped by the social, economic, and legal climates faced by African Americans at different points in history. As the social context changes, so does black philanthropy.

Black philanthropy's past

The roots of black philanthropy can be traced to Africa. It arrived in America with the first slaves, embedded in their cultural and communal traditions of self-help. The pernicious institution of slavery forced Africans from different lands to band together for mutual survival and reinforced their self-help practices.

For African Americans, black philanthropy has been the economic engine that helped them create and sustain the first black mutual aid associations and churches. These institutions, especially the black church, were of special importance during slavery and Jim Crow because their leaders were supported and financed by the African American community. As a result, these leaders were able to voice the concerns of their constituents without fear of economic reprisal, although they were constantly under physical threat and intimidation. Denied access to goods and services from all manner of white institutions, African Americans saw to their own needs through the establishment of their own religious and nonprofit organizations. In many ways, the black church was the first community foundation, aggregating the community's resources across class lines and directing the resources to provide the services and institutions that were needed.

During its earliest years, black philanthropy was directed at social empowerment and transformation. In addition to schools and financial institutions, it gave life to the Underground Railroad and, later, Marcus Garvey's Back to Africa movement and the civil rights movement. Make no mistake; although the various freedom movements received contributions from white donors and their philanthropic institutions, these efforts were predominantly sustained by the lives, volunteer efforts, donations, and money of African Americans.

By 1835, white America had become so afraid of black philanthropy that Virginia, Maryland, and North Carolina had laws banning mutual aid societies and fraternal organizations (Carson, 1993). This is a principal reason that African Americans developed secret societies and nonprofit organizations with dual purposes. One example of a dual-purpose organization is the women's bridge clubs of the South, which had the public purpose of providing social interaction for its members but a secret purpose of engaging in charitable efforts to support the community.

In the face of demeaning, humiliating segregation in which separate was never equal, African American churches and other nonprofit organizations used black philanthropy to turn the impossible into possible and make Martin Luther King Jr.'s dream of an integrated society a reality. In the 1970s, the National Black United Fund won access to the federal workplace campaign as well as to other groups, such as women and the environment.

For three centuries, from the late 1600s to the 1970s, black philanthropy had three defining characteristics. First, African Americans used their collective philanthropy, often through the church, to promote common interests rather than individual interests. Second, black philanthropy was characterized by pooling together relatively modest amounts from multiple individuals rather than relying on a few donors who could give large amounts. Third, black philanthropy was transformative: it was directed at improving the socioeconomic status of African Americans through both self-help and social protest.

Black philanthropy today

Today, black philanthropy is at a crossroads because the African American community is at a crossroads. Fifty years after the momentous *Brown* v. *Board of Education* (1954) decision, things are better for African Americans. Based on the 2000 Census, there are forty-one thousand African American doctors, forty-three thousand African American lawyers, and ninety-one thousand African American engineers. This does not include the large number of African American athletes, entertainers, the new U.S. secretary of state (Condoleezza Rice), the former secretary of state (Colin Powell), or Justice Clarence Thomas. Whether it is broadly acknowledged in the African American community or not, it was King's dream that African Americans would be judged by the content of their character and not the color of their skin.

African Americans today represent the full spectrum of class, wealth, and political ideology. The realization of King's dream has meant that African Americans no longer have identical experiences, and therefore they hold views that are increasingly heterogeneous rather than homogeneous. Although there are those who lament these developments, I would remind them that this is what King, Medgar Evers, and countless others gave their lives to achieve and what millions of African Americans over generations hoped for.

It is equally true that fifty years since *Brown* v. *Board of Education*, African Americans have not yet achieved socioeconomic justice. Consider the following statistics:

- Health outcomes in Harlem, New York, are equal to those of Bangladesh.
- There are more African American men in prison than in college.
- There continues to be ongoing discrimination in corporate America, as evidenced by discrimination suits settled by such corporations as Microsoft, Coca Cola, Eddie Bauer, and Denny's, among others.

Today African Americans no longer share a commonality of experiences even though we share history and skin color. As the axiom would suggest, the focus and direction of black philanthropy are changing. Black philanthropy is more likely to be driven by individual interests rather than communal needs.

This shift is primarily due to three reasons. First, the African American community now has individuals of significant wealth who can make significant gifts consistent with their personal charitable interests. Second, the diminished racial discrimination in America has released African Americans from the burden of having their philanthropy be race focused. Third, black philanthropy is no longer centered through the black church or even other African American nonprofit organizations. Weekly church attendance by African Americans declined from 38 percent in 1970 to 25 percent in 2002 (University of Michigan, n.d.).

More than ever before, black philanthropy reflects what W.E.B. DuBois referred to in *Souls of Black Folks* (1969) as two-ness: the idea that African Americans lived in two worlds—one white, the other black. For many African Americans, these worlds are no longer separate. Music, fashion, and other areas of life that have what is termed crossover appeal, economically and socially, increasingly dominate our society. African Americans increasingly see themselves as part of a global community, and their philanthropy—their time and money—is beginning to reflect these realities. For example, actor Danny Glover and others were arrested in Washington, D.C., in 2004 while protesting the genocide that has occurred in the Sudan.

The future of black philanthropy

The question facing people of African descent in the United States is to what extent we see ourselves as African Americans as opposed to Americanized Africans. African Americans see themselves as having a common history and, more important, an intertwined common destiny. Yet Americanized Africans recognize their common past but see a future in which they are individuals with no obligations or responsibilities to the race. This is not to say that they cannot or will not support African American causes; rather, they do not feel an obligation to have to do so. As the axiom would suggest, the current crossroads has significant implications for the future of black philanthropy. Due to diminished discrimination, more so than at any other point in history, African Americans are free to support their individual interests and pursuits.

Tremendous socioeconomic challenges remain in the African American community. There is an important fundraising case to be made by African American nonprofit organizations focused on traditional civil rights issues inclusive of social justice, education, employment, housing, and health care, among others. These organizations must demonstrate excellence in their programs and their donor relations. Unfortunately, this has not always been the case, as some of these organizations have relied on African Americans to support their organization, even when the service provided has been lacking. Such behavior will no longer be tolerated.

For nonprofit organizations that do not have an African American focus, there exist new opportunities to recruit African American donors in support of their work. To achieve this, these organizations must walk the talk in terms of what they claim to do and deliver excellence in their programming and donor relations. Unlike in decades past, there is more receptivity among African Americans to consider supporting nonprofit organizations that are not focused on African American causes. Nonprofit organizations that want to solicit gifts from African Americans without their input and without boards and staff who fully represent the diversity of the community will ultimately not be successful.

Conclusion

The future of black philanthropy looks brighter than it has ever before. At one end of the spectrum, there is the wonderful example of Oseola McCarty. In 1995, at eighty-seven years of age, McCarty, a washerwoman, donated $150,000 to the University of Southern Mississippi to establish college scholarships; at the time, it was the largest single gift it had ever received ("Oseola McCarty Donates $150,000 to USM," 1995). Later, McCarty stated, "I can't do everything, but I can do something to help somebody. And what I can do, I will do. I wish I could do more." In 2004, Alphonse Fletcher, a thirty-eight-year-old investment professional, announced that he will distribute $50 million in honor of *Brown* v. *Board of Education* (Rimer, 2004). It is worth noting that at age twenty-eight, he gave $4.8 million to Harvard University, his alma mater. These two examples indicate that black philanthropy remains an important community value and is poised to make an even greater impact on America's nonprofit sector in the years ahead.

References

Brown v. *Board of Education of Topeka.* 347 U.S. 483. 1954.

Carson, E. D. *A Hand Up: Black Philanthropy and Self-Help in America.* Washington, D.C.: Joint Center for Political and Economic Studies, 1993.

DuBois, W.E.B. *Souls of Black Folks.* New York: New American Library, 1969. (Originally published 1903.)

NAACP Legal Defense Fund v. *Campbell.* 504 F. Supp. 1365. 1981.

National Black United Fund v. *Campbell.* 494 F. Supp. 748. 1980.

"Oseola McCarty Donates $150,000 to USM." University of Southern Mississippi, press release, July 1995.

Rimer, S. "$50 Million Gift Aims to Build on Legacy of *Brown* v. *Board.*" *New York Times*, May 18, 2004, p. A23.

University of Michigan. *The National Election Studies.* N.d. [www.umich.edu/~nes/].

EMMETT D. CARSON *is president and CEO of the Minneapolis Foundation.*

A veteran black fundraiser challenges blacks in organized philanthropy to embrace the measures of professionalism that will get the benefits of philanthropy focused on suffering and needful black communities.

2

Professionalism in black philanthropy: We have a chance to get it right

Charles R. Stephens

OH, HOW HAPPY I AM that I found the fundraising profession in 1961. If truth be told, this profession really found me. I stumbled into it just as most of my colleagues from that era did. In fact, I was quite upset that I did not get the probation officer's job I had applied for and tested exceptionally well for. I was denied because I had a criminal case pending against me because as a student, I was part of a sit-in. In those days, the state of Georgia made this a felony to discourage the practice, so I was labeled a criminal.

I was not exactly overjoyed when the executive director of the Butler Street YMCA made me the offer to become the YMCA's fundraiser. "Fundraiser?" said I quizzically. "What is that, and what does a fundraiser do?" "Son," said the director, "I think you can do it, and I will be your mentor." When I told my mom and dad about my new position—YMCA membership public relations secretary— and that my primary responsibility was fundraising, they were somewhat less than impressed. It was quite clear that they harbored serious doubts about whether their hard-earned money invested in

NEW DIRECTIONS FOR PHILANTHROPIC FUNDRAISING, NO. 48, SUMMER 2005 © WILEY PERIODICALS, INC.

my college education was money well spent. And I couldn't be too assuring because, in all honesty, I had to tell them that my work was not yet even considered a profession but was, in fact, a developing profession.

Now, here I am, more than forty years later, absolutely happy, an acknowledged fundraising professional, and still engaged. The road to full professional status for fundraising has not been particularly easy and probably still has a few corners to turn to achieve full professional status. The three C's required to bring what we fundraisers do into the arena of profession are a common curriculum, a common code of ethics, and a comprehensively accepted certification. This work has achieved all three, but the caveats are *common* and *comprehensive*. We are still coming to terms with the notion that there can be a comprehensive body of knowledge, a profession-wide enforceable code of ethics, and a common approach to certification standards that covers all of the perceived bases. I am convinced that we are closer than we give ourselves credit for.

Among the professional associations, the Council for Advancement and Support of Education (CASE) has created an excellent, comprehensive curriculum that serves to guide its approach to delivering training programs. This curriculum, I believe, is worthy of being considered profession-wide. The Association of Fundraising Professionals (AFP) has produced an excellent code of ethics with a tested set of enforcement procedures that I believe is worthy of profession-wide consideration. The CFRE (certified fundraising executive) credential, developed in collaboration with most of the major professional associations of fundraisers, is the best candidate for profession-wide acceptance in that arena. So we are almost there.

There have been similar strides toward full professionalism in all of the other areas of work related to nonprofits and philanthropy. There are many excellent training programs. The most storied one, the Fund Raising School, is located at the Center on Philanthropy at Indiana University. There are degrees in nonprofit management and philanthropic studies, and professional associations reflective of practically every category of work related to advancing and managing the philanthropic tradition.

The question now becomes where the black philanthropy professional is in this mix. Who and where are the professionals carrying forward the articulated approaches to managing and bringing into being the nonprofit organizations and approaches required to address critical issues of community in local African American communities and critical issues in regions and the national black community? What is our representation in the professional associations, and how and where do we access the professional training and education that are becoming more and more available and more and more required as more and more people make the conscious decision to pursue careers in the philanthropic sector? Are black professionals making the conscious decision to pursue careers in the philanthropic sector in large enough numbers to make a significant difference?

My review of the available statistics, and they are scarce, cause me great alarm on all of these fronts. For instance, the AFP no longer lists African American membership as a separate item and includes those numbers in a single category labeled "minority." AFP indicates its minority membership at less than 10 percent and its majority membership at 93 percent. I am therefore concluding that the real number for all minorities is 7 percent, which means that African American membership is something less than 7 percent. CASE indicates that of its sixteen thousand members who completed an ethnicity profile, 3 percent identified themselves as black or African American.

On the matter of certification, there also does not seem to be significant interest on the part of African Americans in a fundraising credential. Of 4,379 individuals who are CFRE holders, 37 have identified themselves as African American. Again, this suggests that of two of the C's indicating profession—code of ethics (AFP member or signatory to the AFP code) and credential (CFRE)—African Americans are not significantly represented in either.

I do not mean to suggest that the only black fundraising and nonprofit management professionals are those who affiliate with those organizations or hold the credentials. The groundbreaking research conducted by Alice Green Burnette, "The Privilege to Ask" (a national research and leadership development project that Burnette completed in the late 1990s), makes it quite clear that that is not the case. Burnette's research produced a comprehensive and extensive list of outstanding black professionals, most of whom were not identified with any of the organizations previously mentioned.

I can only conclude that black fundraisers do not value the three C's as measures of professionalism, that these measures are not being aggressively marketed to them, or that accessibility to them is limited. My observations suggest that all of the above represent the current reality, and they all represent a crisis circumstance for getting the benefits of philanthropy, best defined as voluntary action for the public good, focused on suffering and needful black communities.

America's favorite comedian, Bill Cosby, encountered the wrath of some in May 2004 when he spoke out at Constitution Hall in Washington, D.C., about some persistent issues of community facing African Americans, particularly challenges that African American youth are facing. He spoke in his own inimitable way, and many of us did not like what he had to say and the way he said it. Many also did not care too much for where he said it. But all of us know, deep within, that what he had to say was true.

Our challenge, and America's challenge, is to develop and implement the strategies to do whatever has to be done to bring about the sea change required to make these wrongs right.

We continue in crisis in the effort to bring about healthy community in urban black communities in spite of the tremendous progress we have made as a race in all of the conceivable areas of achievement. The crisis is exacerbated by the fact that there is increasing distance between the haves and the have-nots in our community, and there is increased resentment and the continuing movement toward the development of a permanent underclass that presents major problems for all levels of society. These issues must be more aggressively addressed, and they must be aggressively addressed now.

I believe very firmly that voluntary action for the public good represents the best and only hope for effectively addressing some of the long-standing issues that continue to fuel the current circumstance of racial and ethnic divisiveness in the United States. I believe the expiation of those issues is dependent on actualizing strong, personalized neighborhood-based, neighborhood-led, neighborhood-focused, and neighborhood-supported programs that draw on the knowledge and experience of professionally trained nonprofit fundraisers and nonprofit managers. We must find a way to significantly ramp up the number of black professionals who choose the philanthropic sector as their life's work. We are in a circumstance now where employing trained African American philanthropy professionals means attracting them from other needful black organizations. As more majority institutions and programs come to terms with the growing diversity of our nation, this shortage of talent will become more and more acute. We desperately need the focus and insight that black philanthropy professionals could bring to the unique circumstances found in troubled African American urban communities.

How do we produce these professionals? I believe a major problem is that none of the 116 historically black colleges and universities in our nation have programs focusing on career opportunities in philanthropy. This must change. We need a collaborative effort between the member colleges of the College Fund/UNCF, the Thurgood Marshall Scholarship Fund member institutions, the Association of Black Foundation Executives, and the Nonprofit Academic Centers Council to remedy this situation. The African American community and America need historically black colleges producing people trained to build community in the too many places where hope is a rapidly disappearing commodity. This is a key first step.

Anybody who has ever done any nonprofit fundraising and nonprofit programming knows that these activities work only when there is some level of infrastructure to access, even if the infrastructure is only rudimentary. In African American communities, that infrastructure is most likely going to be anchored by an African American church.

I believe a huge partnership opportunity exists for the National Center on Black Philanthropy, the National Black United Fund, the Association of Black Foundation Executives, and the Institute for Church Administration and Management. It could be seminal in helping to continue to expand the transformation of depressed communities and engender hope and healing among populations that currently are the subject of much head shaking and hand wringing.

In my view, these organizations, in a collaborative working relationship, could be the vanguard for helping church social ministries spin off these ministries into viable nonprofits. These could become capable of attracting broad-based support and helping neighborhood-based nonprofits and neighbor initiatives move toward nonprofit status to be more effective in addressing issues of community empowerment and healing.

I applaud the currently existing collaboration between the Fund Raising School, the Lilly Endowment, and the Thurgood Marshall Scholarship Fund to provide development training for fundraising and other professionals at public historically black colleges and universities and for alumni fundraising training. These programs ultimately will serve to deepen the pool of black fundraising and nonprofit management professionals, but the immediate need is much greater than our current training capacity can meet. We need a creative, innovative, massive, collaborative, national plan of attack.

We need a national association of black fundraising and nonprofit management professionals that could enter into collaboration with the Association of Fundraising Professionals and the various certification entities to ensure that relevant professional growth and credentialing opportunities are accessible to black professionals.

We have the opportunity to get it right. We have a strong cadre of trained philanthropy professionals, but we do not have nearly enough. We have professional infrastructure, but that infrastructure could be far more effective through imaginative, focused collaborations.

We are a $600 billion annual economy, we have Fortune 500 CEOs, we have multimillion-dollar black-owned businesses, we have foundations and foundation executives, and we are moving rapidly and steadily to build personal wealth. Most important, we have the commitment to go back and give back that defines the earliest days of our presence in this nation and continues to define us today.

We are a philanthropic people. We have a chance to get professionalism in black philanthropy right, and we must do so. For the memory of our mothers and fathers, we must get it right. For the memory and in honor of our grandmothers and grandfathers who sacrificed to do good, we must get it right. For the cousins who were not real cousins who just needed a helping hand, we must get it right. For those in our communities who have neither hope nor hope of hope, we must get it right. And in the words of Senator Barack Obama, in honor of "the audacity of hope," we must get it right. We can and we must do all that is required to get it right.

CHARLES R. STEPHENS *is managing partner of Skystone Ryan, an international fundraising consulting firm.*

*The African American megachurch is responding
to the challenges of modern society by using the tools
of secular success: economic development, political
clout, and social responsibility.*

3

The African American megachurch: Giving and receiving

Cheryl Hall-Russell

FROM SMALL MEETING HOUSES nestled into southern rural towns
to $25 million megachurches in some of America's largest cities,
the African American church has undergone dramatic changes. The
changes not only affect the edifices in which parishioners worship;
they can also be seen in the way African Americans view their spiritual institutions and how they use their social and political capital.

This chapter looks at the evolution of the African American
megachurch, defined for this research as churches with twenty-five
hundred or more active members. Information from forty-one
African American megachurches was collected, including geo-
graphical and membership statistics, outreach services, economic
development investment, and, when available, annual budgets.
While not inclusive of all African American megachurches, the data
collected gave a good idea of growth trends, social outreach emphasis, and spiritual and theological philosophies.

Questions focused on church growth, philanthropic traditions,
outreach programs that are currently in place, and challenges facing
the church. These key areas were examined:

NEW DIRECTIONS FOR PHILANTHROPIC FUNDRAISING, NO. 48, SUMMER 2005 © WILEY PERIODICALS, INC.

- Why African Americans attend megachurches
- When the church experienced its greatest growth
- What the predominant socioeconomic class is of new members
- How philanthropic values are taught in the church
- What outreach programs are being promoted by the church

There were also questions concerning demographic and financial status. Notable changes have occurred in the six years since the initial research was conducted. The Church of God in Christ has almost doubled in size, and the number of African American megachurches with memberships over fifteen thousand has increased dramatically.

Defining the black church

African American spiritual institutions began their existence as separate entities because of the forces of racial discrimination that made African Americans worship separately from whites. The term *black church* refers to those churches attended by a majority of African Americans, and they vary in terms of denominations. Although the black church is not a formal body, similarities in worship patterns and roles in the black community resulted in this simple blanket term. In reality, the black church is far from simple, and the African American megachurch represents one of the more complex changes to happen to the black church.

The evolution of the black church began in the late 1700s and early 1800s. The oldest denominations developed before the Emancipation Proclamation when Richard Allen, disgusted with his treatment in the white Methodist church, started the African Methodist Episcopal church in 1787. Other new denominations soon followed (see Table 3.1).

As African Americans began to migrate in large numbers out of the South toward jobs in the North, they took their religious traditions with them. New black churches began to pop up all over the country. Today there are approximately seventy-five thousand

Table 3.1. African American Denominations

Denomination	Established	Total Membership (approximate)
African Methodist Episcopal Church	1787	2.5 million members, 8,000 churches
African Methodist Episcopal Church Zion	1796	1.28 million members, 3,125 churches
Christian Methodist Episcopal Church	1870	1 million members 2,063 churches
Church of God in Christ	1907	8 million members, 10,500 churches
National Baptist Convention USA	1886	5 million members, 33,000 churches
National Baptist Convention of America	1915	3.5 million members, 12,336 churches
Progressive National Baptist Convention	1961	2.5 million members, 1,800 churches

African American churches in the United States (Billingsley, 1992). They are largely decentralized, allowing new churches to proliferate with little local or national-level interference.

From the neighborhood to the forum

Toward the end of the 1980s, researchers began to take notice of the rise of the black megachurch. Interestingly, the phenomenon of the megachurch began for both the black and the traditionally white church at around the same time. Researchers at the Hartford Institute for Religion Research report that nearly all megachurches were founded after 1955. Their explosive growth occurred in the mid-1980s and continues today (Thumma, n.d.).

The African American middle class continues to be drawn into these new Christian epicenters by charismatic, high-profile ministers; spirit-filled worship services; music; networking potential; and numerous support systems ("Black Megachurches Surge," 1996). Worshippers are also attracted to a new generation of African

American clergy, who are often better educated than their pulpit predecessors. In the best tradition of the historic black church, the African American megachurch continues to offer sociological benefits to its members by empowerment that provides freedom, control, and a sense of belonging—feelings often denied minorities in the United States.

Quite a few black megachurches are part of the neo-Pentecostal movement. These churches are usually led by conservative charismatic pastors whose approach to conventional doctrine does not sit well within the confines of the traditional church. An example of this change can be seen in the Full Gospel Baptist Church Fellowship. A fast-growing denomination, its founder, Bishop Paul Morton, broke with the traditional Baptist church when he embraced the power of spiritual gifts. The movement has since exploded and touts the tagline, "The movement that gives Baptists the right to choose." Greater St. Stephen's Full Gospel Church in New Orleans is now one of the largest black megachurches in the nation, with over twenty thousand members.

Other nondenominational megachurches began to flourish in the late 1980s and early 1990s. Creflo Dollar's World Changers ministry exploded on the scene from its home in College Park, Georgia. It is now a multimillion-dollar megaplex with a large television ministry. With a membership of eighteen thousand, the church employs over five hundred and has multiple outreach ministries.

The same can be said for another megachurch movement: the eighteen-thousand-member Potters House, in Dallas, Texas. Led by West Virginia–born T. D. Jakes, this ministry has had nationwide influence. T. D. Jakes Ministries is its own multimillion-dollar company with sales of CDs, books, and videotapes, as well as national and international conferences. Another undeniable force is the ministry of Reverend Kenneth Ulmer and the Faithful Central Bible Church in Inglewood, California. With seventeen hundred members in 1993, the church has grown to eleven thousand members and recently purchased the Great Western Forum (formerly home of the Los Angeles Lakers) as its new worship center.

Changing philosophy

As megachurches begin to change the landscape of the traditional black church, it is clear that there has also been a change in philosophy in terms of the role of the church. This has been a source of contention in the black spiritual community, with charges of middle-class blacks running away from their roots to shiny suburban churches or that they are forgetting their social and civic duties and turning to "prosperity preaching" instead of lifting up the poor and disenfranchised and focusing on civil rights. Questions have arisen questioning where the black megachurch is in terms of philanthropic outreach and if it is willing and able to respond to social ills.

Because of the challenges of modern society, the black church is finding that it is difficult to respond with philanthropic outreach in the same way it used to. In the 1950s and 1960s, the challenges in the black community could more easily be linked to two major factors, racism and poverty, and the obvious relationship between the two. As times have changed, threats to the black community have also changed. Early challenges focused on secularization, racism, inadequate funding, and uneducated or undereducated clergy. Our more recent research found similar responses and more modern problems, including an increasingly disconnected lower class, single parenthood, crumbling neighborhoods, and concerns about church relevance.

The response of African American megachurches has been to broaden its mission by focusing on the tools of secular success: economic development, political savvy, and social responsibility (Burch, 2002). They recognize that unlike a generation ago, many of their members were previously unchurched. These members are often young and new to the teaching of the church, and leaders have felt a need to tailor their messages and focus to areas they feel are more relevant to this generation. While not completely ignoring the social and class issues pressing in on the African American population, many of these churches are populated by the African

American middle class, whose focus can be very different from that of the lower class.

Megachurches in the survey had several areas of philanthropic and social outreach that evidenced the change in the type of support being lent to the community. When asked about their outreach ministries, most had basic food pantries, substance abuse and relationship counseling, and emergency services. The internal ministries like usher boards, drama, choirs, parking lot aides, rites of passage, and men and women's groups far outnumbered outreach. Many of the churches were involved in economic development: home repairs, senior housing, job creation, and commercial development, for example. Many held regular seminars on finance, credit repair, and investment strategies.

Several African American megachurches have taken their new roles as community developers to a new level. Recently the retired senior pastor of the First African Methodist Episcopal (FAME) in Los Angeles, Reverend Cecil Murray, spearheaded the development of housing units targeted at low- to moderate-income individuals. The FAME Renaissance organization operates several major social and business development programs designed to create wealth in impoverished communities within Los Angeles County.

One of the most ambitious projects to be taken on by an African American megachurch is being put forth by the Windsor United Methodist Church in Houston. Its senior pastor, Kirbyjon Caldwell, who received an M.B.A. from the Wharton School, has spearheaded the Pyramid Community Development Corporation. It developed the Power Center, a complex completed in 1995 that consists of two buildings totaling 104,000 square feet on 24 acres of land. It also has under construction Corinthian Point, a housing and retail community. When completed, the subdivision will include 452 single-family homes. This is the one of the largest real estate ventures ever undertaken by a nonprofit organization.

These megachurch leaders have embraced the idea that economic stability in the United States is key to growth in all areas. While this is a concept that is hard to argue with, some harsh criticism has been launched at churches that preach what has been called "prosperity gospel." The theory behind this approach is if you are right with God and seed into his church, you will become prosperous. Megachurch leaders like Creflo Dollar at World Changers in Atlanta and Fred Price with Crenshaw Christian Center in Los Angeles teach their congregants that God did not call his children to a life of poverty (Hadnot, 2004). Dollar said in a 2000 sermon, "I've heard people in church say, 'I may not have this, I may not have that, but praise the Lord when I get to heaven on the other side.' Well, honey, God wants you to get it on this side" (Hadnot, 2004). His approach is not unique. Megachurch leaders throughout the country have adopted this style. Often tithing, or giving 10 percent of earned income to the church, is cited as a way to ensure personal prosperity. Fredrick Harris, a political scientist at the University of Rochester in Rochester, New York, stated, "The message has moved from community empowerment to individual prosperity. The thinking is that if individuals rise, so will the rest of the community. That is a complete reversal from the mission of the black church during slavery, Reconstruction and civil rights" (Hadnot, 2004).

Recurring trends

Commonalities became apparent in the churches we studied:

- The middle class making up the bulk of the membership
- Strong emphasis on bringing males back into the church
- A message of economic freedom
- The development and support of black businesses
- The neo-Pentecostal movement as a large factor

African American megachurches from coast to coast connect their continued growth to several general factors:

- Strong charismatic pastoral leaders seen as visionaries or prophets
- Conservative theology

- New physical church structures
- Strong music ministries
- Multiple services
- A smorgasbord of services and ministries

The future of the African American megachurch

The African American megachurch is a powerful fixture in many communities. Far from fading, these institutions continue to grow at a rapid pace, leaving their marks on large urban communities throughout the United States. Many of these churches are performing phenomenal outreach. Others are still struggling with their rapid expansion and the challenges that are inherent in that growth. Many of the megachurches that started out in poor minority communities have moved to the suburbs and have become commuter churches for inner-city residents. A few critics of the megachurch feel that these institutions have become very self-serving. Fortunately, for those dependent on the philanthropy of the church, current approaches seem to blend the two schools of thought: it is all right to have an affluent lifestyle as long as one remembers "that those to whom much is given, much is expected."

There will always be a fear that the bubble will burst on African American megachurches. These structures, so dependent on charismatic leaders, risk stability when a change of leadership is required. The push to build larger and larger structures also poses a threat if costs are not contained and debt outstrips income. It is not yet known when a church has grown so much that it reaches a critical mass and can no longer serve its members as individuals. Many of the more strategic megachurches have adopted church systems that encourage the opening of satellite churches, or "seed" churches, to accommodate extreme growth patterns.

It is obvious that the African American megachurch is having a major effect on the communities it serves. The forty-one churches we looked at represent over 369,714 members around the nation. They own almost a half-billion dollars in real estate and represent eleven denominations. Only time will tell whether this growth will continue or if African Americans will begin a reverse migration back to neighborhood-based churches. Critics will continue to hammer the megachurch for its perceived failure to maintain close connections to its social and political agendas. In a rapidly changing environment, it will be important to continue to watch the trends being established by these new behemoths to see if they are able to sustain their remarkable appeal.

Referencess

Billingsley, A. *Climbing Jacob's Ladder*. New York: Simon & Schuster, 1992.
"Black Megachurches Surge." *Christian Century*, 1996, 7(21), 686–687.
Burch, A. "Black Churches' New Calling." *Miami Herald*, Feb., 2002.
Hadnot, I. J. "Some Black Churches Shun Politics." *Dallas Morning News*, Aug. 4, 2004.
Thumma, S. "Exploring the Megachurch Phenomena: Their Characteristics and Cultural Context." N.d. [http://hirr.hartsem.edu/bookshelf/thumma_article2.html].

CHERYL HALL-RUSSELL *directs the Urban Mission Branch of the YMCA of Greater Indianapolis.*

In-person interviews with New York City–area donors reveal significant changes in black philanthropy and sharp differences between generations that came of age before the civil rights era and those who were born later.

4

Philanthropy among African American donors in the New York metropolitan region: A generational analysis

Felinda Mottino, Eugene D. Miller

THE AIM OF THE DONOR RESEARCH PROJECT (DRP) is to add to the existing scholarship on philanthropy in emerging communities in the New York metropolitan region. The project has three stages: literature reviews, analysis of demographic and economic data, and donor interviews. Donor interviews are meant to help nonprofit organizations understand their contributors so they can serve them better and be more effective partners for their philanthropic

The Donor Research Project was conducted at the Center on Philanthropy and Civil Society, City University of New York Graduate Center, in conjunction with the Coalition for New Philanthropy in New York, a promotion of a philanthropy initiative of five partnering organizations: the Asian American Federation of New York, the Hispanic Federation, the New York Regional Association of Grantmakers, the Twenty First Century Foundation, and the Center on Philanthropy and Civil Society. Funding for this research was provided by the Ford Foundation, the Carnegie Corporation of New York, and the coalition.

NEW DIRECTIONS FOR PHILANTHROPIC FUNDRAISING, NO. 48, SUMMER 2005 © WILEY PERIODICALS, INC.

efforts, as well as to learn how to increase support. The DRP has examined philanthropy in the African American, Asian American, and Latino communities; this chapter focuses on the African American community.

The changing demographic and economic environment

Why is it important to study donors in communities of color? According to the 2000 Census, New York City no longer has one majority population. Instead, the white, non-Hispanic community has fallen to slightly over one-third of the entire population of the five boroughs of the city, while the Latino community has increased to about 25 percent, and African Americans maintain about another 25 percent of the total. Surprisingly, primarily due to immigration, by 2000 nearly 10 percent of New Yorkers were Asian American, and this population continues to grow (Scott, 2001). Suburban counties reflect similar patterns of change, and these long-term trends are projected to increase over time both within the region and nationally (Chen, 2001; U.S. Bureau of the Census, 1990, 2000). The phenomenon of an inner city of color surrounded by an affluent white community is much more complicated and nuanced around major metropolitan areas such as New York, San Francisco, and Washington, D.C.

In addition, the human, social, and financial capital of African Americans, Asian Americans, and Latinos is increasing. While still below the average for white non-Hispanic households and businesses, entrepreneurialism, business revenues, household income, home ownership, and attainment of college degrees are growing at faster rates. In New York City, from 1990 to 2000, household income increased (in adjusted dollars) 13 percent for African Americans, 15 percent for Asians, and 8 percent for Latinos (New York City Housing and Vacancy Survey, 1991, 1999).

Home ownership levels for twenty-three counties surrounding New York City grew as well: 29 percent for African Americans, 80 percent for Asians, and 56 percent for Latinos (U.S. Bureau of the

Census, 1990, 2000). Correspondingly, these communities also experienced high rates of growth in educational attainment. For example, the number of individuals in these communities achieving bachelor's degrees has grown dramatically. For African Americans, the increase was 119 percent, for Asian Americans 221 percent, and for Latinos 146 percent (U.S. Bureau of the Census, 2000; the rate of increase in education is for individuals twenty-five years of age and older with college degrees and includes absolute growth).

What do these trends mean for the future of philanthropy in general and black philanthropy in particular? This chapter examines the work undertaken by the DRP and sheds light on how and to what extent the focus of African American giving is changing. (In this chapter, we use the term *African American* interchangeably with *black* to mean persons who self-identified as African American or black. We include people who were born in Africa, the Caribbean, and the United States.)

The Donor Research Project

This research is based on 166 face-to-face interviews conducted with donors in the African American, Asian American, and Latino communities in metropolitan New York in 2002–2003. Efforts were made to introduce a level of randomness into the process of selecting interviewees. To do so, we worked with fourteen community-based nonprofit organizations in New York City, requesting and receiving access to their donor lists. To fill gaps and provide a more representative sample of donors, we also employed a modified snowball approach to identify donors for interview. In the end, we interviewed fifty-eight African American donors, fifty-five Asian American donors, and fifty-three Latino donors. (The study, which aimed to interview at least fifty donors from each ethnic group, used a stratified sample.) Donors were asked about their views of philanthropy, their philanthropic dreams, the two largest gifts made by their household in the year prior to the interview, and decision making and advisement surrounding donations. This chapter is based on interviews with the fifty-eight African American donors.

Data analysis was an inductive process to identify motivations and intent and their relation to patterns of giving, and to demographic and situational factors. Wherever possible, we situate donors within the larger demographic and economic picture provided by census data. Although every effort was made to select interview respondents representatively, this is not a true random sample of donors of color. Therefore, inferences must be drawn with caution; they are suggestive of trends among growing populations and emerging subgroups.

Early in the research, we realized that the donor's age affected his or her philanthropic perspective, which also made sense from a historical perspective. Accordingly, we divided the African American community into older and younger generations (pre– and post–civil rights legislation), with the dividing line being those born in or before 1963 and those born after. The reasoning is that those in the younger group, who came of age in the 1980s, are beneficiaries of the ensuing legislation, including the 1964 Civil Rights Act, affirmative action legislation, and the 1965 Immigration Reform Act. And as beneficiaries, it is reasonable to expect that they have had increased access to opportunities (first educational and then occupational) and that their philanthropic ideas and behaviors might differ from those of preceding generations.

The sample

Of the fifty-eight African Americans in the study, 34 percent were from post–civil rights generations (under the age of forty) and 66 percent from pre–civil rights generations (age forty or above). Among the older donors there were more women (61 percent), and in the younger group there were more men (65 percent). All the donors interviewed in the study had at least a bachelor's degree. Among the younger donors, 20 percent had already earned graduate degrees, primarily in business. Among the older donors, 89 percent had graduate degrees in a variety of areas, including social work, medicine, law, and business.

Older donors tended to work in the nonprofit sector, mostly in social service professions; only 29 percent worked in the private for-profit sector, while 66 percent worked in the private nonprofit sector, and another 5 percent in government or the public sector. Compared to the larger New York City population of African Americans with a bachelor's degree or higher education, the proportion of our donors working in the private for-profit sector (50 percent) is comparable overall to the larger population (45 percent). However, when broken down by age group, older African Americans are underrepresented (29 percent) and younger African Americans are overrepresented (90 percent). Clearly, there is a strong shift away from employment in nonprofit and government work. (Census data indicate growing numbers of people under age forty working in the private sector across all ethnic groups.) Younger African Americans we interviewed tended to be starting or building careers in financial services, including banks and Wall Street investment firms.

African Americans in the study reported household income from all sources to be between $50,000 and $999,000 per year for both the older and younger groups. The median category for the entire group was $100,000 to $149,000; for the older group taken alone, the median category was $150,000 to $199,000. Looking at income another way, 71 percent overall reported an annual income of at least $100,000; among the younger group, it was 55 percent and among the older, 79 percent. According to census data, median income levels of DRP donors surpass New York City median incomes (black and white).

Gifts

Overall household giving among African Americans in the study in the year prior to the interview ranged from $200 to $40,000, with a median of $5,250 and a mean of $8,147. This surpasses the national average of $3,976 (adjusted mean of giving in 2000 from contributing households with incomes of at least $100,000; INDE-PENDENT SECTOR, 2001) and, along with other research, helps dispel the notion that African Americans as well as other people of color are simply recipients of giving and not active philanthropists (Anft and Lipman, 2003). We asked donors in detail about their two largest gifts in the year preceding the interview. What follows is a discussion of those gifts in terms of size, community of interest, philanthropic targets, and motivation. Data are presented in a comparative generational framework.

Size of largest gifts

Older African Americans gave between $250 and $20,000 as their largest gift, with a median of $3,000 and a mean of $4,490. Younger African Americans gave largest gifts between $100 and $10,000, with a median of $875 and a mean of $1,774. (The interview criterion was at least $200, but during the interview, three younger donors recalled giving a top gift of less than $200 in the previous year.)

Community of interest

Interviewees were asked, "How do you define the community or communities you intend your charitable giving to help?" Some people had a clear priority or emphasized a particular community. However, most named one community and then went on to name several others.

In the analyses, we sought to determine to what extent donors focus their philanthropy on their own ethnic community, and we identified expanding circles of interest. In the innermost circle, we placed donors most focused on their own ethnic community, that is, those who had a clear priority (such as, "My community of interest is the African American community"), as well as those who led with or emphasized their ethnic community. In the next circle, we showed those who included their community by name as the second or third priority. In the third, more expanded, circle, we added those who named a more expansive community, such as people of color, minorities, inner-city areas, "the disenfranchised"—in other words, groups traditionally underserved. The last circle brought in those who expressed an interest in any people in need: youth, elderly, homeless, and others. Responses were nuanced, and both older and younger groups ended up wanting to help people in need, but they arrived by different routes: older donors tended to start off with their own ethnic community, while younger donors began with a more expanded idea of community before focusing on their own ethnic group.

Among the pre–civil rights (older) generation of African Americans, 45 percent led with "African American" community. Many had clear priorities focused on specific areas. Five percent included the African American community by name as second or third priority. Another 34 percent mentioned communities of color, the marginalized, or the underprivileged, indicating a strong interest in groups traditionally underserved. Sixteen percent responded that they wanted to help "people in need," "the neighborhood," and so forth. Adding these percentages shows that 100 percent focused on some group or groups in need of resources.

Among younger African Americans, 25 percent led with "African American," and another 10 percent mentioned African Americans or the African American community by name as one of their priorities. Thirty-five percent mentioned communities of color, minority, or the underprivileged. Thirty percent mentioned needy persons. As with older generations of African Americans, 100 percent of this group intends for their philanthropy to help those without access and to work toward greater equality of opportunity but with less focus on racial or ethnic background.

This marks an important departure from traditional approaches in black philanthropy. Historically, philanthropy was directed to family and, by extension, to a community that was racially and ethnically defined. Younger African American donors in our study expressed a more expansive understanding of community beyond race and ethnicity to include community of need. However, the broader concept of community is linked, as we will see, with a strong focus on education, which is often tailored by a more restrictive idea about who should be the recipients of the gifts. Rather than going to uplift the community in general, many see giving as more strategic, where the largesse should be directed to providing resources (particularly education) to those most able to benefit from them and uplift the community.

Recipient organizations

Recipient organizations are those to which donors in the study gave their top two largest monetary gifts. The organizations have been grouped into (1) churches, (2) educational institutions and programs, (3) groups other than religious or educational that serve the community, (4) international organizations, and (5) other, including mainstream, organizations.

Older Generations. In most cases, the top two gifts were given to charitable organizations in the United States, with some going to international programs and a few going to political campaigns. Organizations most likely to receive one of the top gifts from older African Americans were churches. Church giving was followed by giving to education (school or college plus educational programs), as well as to other noneducational organizations serving the black community.

More than half of the older African American donors (55 percent) gave one of their two largest gifts to a local church or religious appeal. Many African Americans made it clear that they see the church not only as a religious and spiritual place but also as a center for community development. Their gifts to church are inspired as much by their desire to see economic and social development as by their religious commitments.

Nearly one-third gave to a school or educational program. Most of these (21 percent) gave to a U.S. college, university, or high school; 13 percent gave to alma maters, including both mainstream universities and one historically black university. Eleven percent gave to educational funds or programs, including the United Negro College Fund, Sponsors for Educational Opportunity, Student Sponsor Partnership, and National Student Partners.

About one-quarter (21 percent) gave one of their two largest gifts to an organization (other than education) serving the local or national African American community. These included the National Urban League, a black fraternity, the Twenty-First Century Foundation, African American Women's Fund, and local organizations.

Twenty-four percent gave to organizations serving people of color or inner-city neighborhoods. In addition, 8 percent gave to organizations that serve women or the gay community.

Far higher than the mainstream average (according to *Giving USA 2003*, only 1.9 percent of total estimated giving went to international affairs), there were 13 percent who gave to an international program, project, or cause. Most were located in Africa or the Caribbean.

Twenty-nine percent of older-generation African Americans also gave to black politicians, the American Public Health Association, the National Association of Social Workers, a day nursery, a nursing home, a track club, and other local organizations.

Younger Generations. As people who are leaving school and starting a career, many younger donors turn their philanthropic efforts back to the educational institutions and programs that helped and supported them. For younger African Americans, the most popular gifts were to educational institutions. About one-third (30 percent) gave to their alma maters, including two historically black colleges. Nearly two-thirds (60 percent) gave to an educational program. Three people gave to two educational programs: one in which they had participated and a second one.

There were not as many younger as older African Americans who gave one of their largest gifts to church. Among the younger group, it was 30 percent. And because of the focus on educational programs, there were fewer larger gifts for noneducational community programs.

Similar to older African Americans, 15 percent gave to an international program, project, or cause. One was located in Africa, and another was described as having a connection to South Africa; one was a mainstream international organization.

Younger-generation African Americans also gave to the American Cancer Society, the American Heart Association, people on the street, and local organizations.

Here again we see a measurable divergence from traditional giving patterns. Older African Americans focused their giving on church, community organizations, and education. For younger African Americans, church giving remained strong, but they made education (both schools and educational programs) their top priority. As Carson (1990) and others have made clear, the black church has been central to African American philanthropy as both a sanctuary for worship and a place to channel resources for social, economic, and political development. However, education is paramount among the young and strongly linked to careers in business and finance. The younger generations seem to be balancing traditional philanthropic responsibilities with a contemporary understanding of philanthropy as a vehicle that facilitates individual opportunity through mainstream paths.

Inspiration

We asked donors, "What is the one most important underlying inspiration for your philanthropy, such as a person, religion, philosophy, emotion, event, or purpose?" Their answers reflected that philanthropy is a repository of traditional values passed from one generation to the next, and the transference clearly overcomes a range of disruptions. At the same time, ways in which successive generations interpret and operationalize these practices reflect changes in the broader society and differences in the career paths and opportunities afforded different individuals. Our purpose in asking donors to discuss their underlying inspiration for giving was in part to differentiate traditional motives of giving from contemporary expressions more sharply.

The themes that emerged from our analysis were five broad categories of inspiration: "Proper Thing to Do," "Give Back," "Uplift Others," "It's Satisfying," and "It Connects Me with . . . ". Of these, we found that "Proper Thing to Do" and "It's Satisfying" are characterized by traditional values. Examination of "Give Back," "Uplift Others," and "It Connects Me with . . . " across the generations reveals something new—a different kind of motivation growing out of traditional practice but responding to contemporary conditions.

"Proper Thing to Do." All African American donors expressed very similar sentiments. Almost half of each group, younger and older, said that what inspired them to give was that it was the right thing to do, based on what they learned from parents, church, religious philosophies, or the example of others who give. Many older African Americans emphasized a family history of giving for religious and philosophical but also humanitarian reasons.

Younger African American donors have much in common with older generations. They said their parents taught them to give and instilled the importance of giving. Some cited religious teachings, and one said that what inspires him is "what my faith tells me about giving and issues of service in general."

"Give Back." Older donors spoke more generally about giving back to the community. Younger donors wanted to give back to the specific school or program that helped them succeed.

A younger African American donor explained, "I was lucky to be born to my parents and to get to come here [current job]. Realizing that I'm not responsible for my own success, therefore when I do succeed, I have to try to make sure that somebody else gets that [help] with the understanding that they will [also] have to give back." Here, giving back is more narrowly focused to create individual rather than communal opportunities.

"Uplift Others." Among older African Americans, uplift was related to a sense of the spiritual, giving back, community development, and providing for the next generation. Several cited the importance of the United Negro College Fund. The emphasis was on "taking care of the whole family," as stated by one of the participants:

We as people of color must consistently be strong in our efforts and convictions in reaching back and making a way to providing greater opportunity to the next generation. There was a point in time when that was our spiritual philosophy, but we got lost somewhere. . . . We bought a bill of goods from somebody and I don't know if we started thinking we were mainstream or what. The reality is that a couple of generations have suffered as a result of us not taking care of the whole family—it takes a village to raise a child. . . . So my philosophy is [about] how do you provide for/give that next generation that opportunity to climb up and succeed.

For young professionals, there was a focus on "uplift the disadvantaged" (helping poor and minorities get fair treatment, access, opportunities and often with an articulated awareness of poverty, disenfranchisement, inequalities, and so forth). However, donors in this group often wanted to focus on helping out one individual at a time, especially those individuals who could contribute the most or go the furthest with their educations and careers.

"It's Satisfying." Giving is emotional and self-satisfying; it gives meaning to life and is personally empowering. It allows people to feel proud of their accomplishments in a positive way. Younger and older generations expressed similar sentiments of pride and satisfaction when giving, and both reflected on the benefits of seeing directly the results of their giving (through mentorships or other hands-on activities).

"It Connects Me with . . ." Both groups spoke about how philanthropy connects them to something beyond themselves. Although they used similar language, the experience appeared quite different, and in some ways one was actually the reverse of the other. For the younger generations, philanthropy kept them connected to communities they were leaving. It provided a kind of self-validation. Some young professionals used philanthropy to establish a connection with community and to anchor themselves.

For some older African Americans (though this is across generations as well), there was a special connection to traditional African American neighborhoods, such as Harlem. One respondent explained her connection to Harlem as follows: "I came to Harlem in the 1970s and then came back 10 years later. Harlem had been portrayed in the media as this negative, violent, drug-infested community but I knew better. I knew about the strengths in the community and I felt there ought to be ways to praise and validate the unsung heroes and heroines of the community."

Social justice and political involvement

The desire to effect fundamental social change has long been a significant element of black philanthropy. From the resistance to slavery to the political struggles of the civil rights and black nationalism eras, black philanthropy has helped establish and maintain many organizations to promote change. This remains the case. Whatever their specific underlying motivation, all the donors we interviewed, young and old and across ethnic lines, expressed a strong desire to effect social change and a clear sense that they hoped their philanthropy would address root causes of social ills. They frequently spoke about injustice, the lack of access, and how these difficulties, experienced by preceding generations, should not have to be suffered again. Both older and younger donors identified with the need to eliminate past injustices because they or someone close to them experienced them firsthand. This said, there is significant disaffection with the political system, especially among the post–civil rights generations.

A number of young donors in particular take a holistic approach, seeing the interconnections of social phenomena. One stated, "What troubles me the most, in this country . . . each different group in society has different access to resources, the basic resources: education, housing, health care. . . . And it has a snowball effect, I mean, if you don't get a good education then you won't be able to get a good job and then you don't have money so you can't afford health insurance, etc."

To get a gauge on the level of formal political engagement, we asked donors the total amount their household had contributed to political parties and candidates. Not all donors gave political contributions. Some people who said they did not make a political contribution the year prior to the interview said they make donations other years, especially during major campaigns. Others told us that they never give to politics.

More than half of the older African Americans recalled making a political contribution in the year preceding the interview. Only 20 percent of the younger generations did so. A number of younger donors had negative views of political giving or simply preferred to focus their efforts in other directions.

Our findings coincide with those of Gibson (2001) and Fields (2003), who found that young people, working together across lines of ethnic and racial difference, are interested in change and that they participate in community service but not in politics. The young donors we have interviewed tend not to trust the government's ability to solve community problems. Their idea of social change is to put to use their business acumen to assist, educate, and advance individuals of color or others in need, especially those with talent and ambition, so that they can become key players in the financial services industry, which they see as the most powerful sector in terms of influencing not only the U.S. and international economy, but also U.S. political and social agendas. The following comment by a black Latino captures the perception of the financial industry among many of the younger donors:

Working in this [financial] industry you see around you that it's probably one of the best-kept secrets as it relates to career paths. And you look around you don't see African Americans, you don't see Latinos, you don't see as many women and I believe this industry drives the U.S. economy more than people can imagine. The ability to influence and to make a difference is phenomenal when you understand what's going on in the capital markets and if you understand what's going on on Wall Street, . . . and if we don't get access to that, then it just continues to retard our ability to have a significant impact.

Conclusion

This chapter has examined the giving practices of African Americans through a generational lens: those born before or in 1963 and those born after. We think that this is an important distinction. The younger generations represent an emerging group—one that has reaped the benefits of the political struggles of the 1950s, 1960s, and early 1970s and is relatively well positioned to both achieve wealth and exercise philanthropic influence. (This is not to say that the objectives of the civil rights, the women's movement, and other related movements have reached completion. It is to underscore that the movements have made tangible gain.)

Our research reveals a trend: while black philanthropy remains committed to establishing and maintaining black institutions, advantage—for individuals and the community as a whole—is seen in using philanthropic dollars to open pathways to broadly based, and in some cases elite, societal institutions.

Whatever the specific underlying motivation, the donors we interviewed (young and old and across racial and ethnic lines) expressed a strong desire to effect social change. They consistently spoke about injustice and the lack of access, and how these difficulties, experienced by preceding generations, should not have to be suffered again. Many reflected acute awareness of the conflict and struggles of the past.

However, this commitment to advance social change did not translate into consistent financial support for political candidates and parties. Nor did many speak of championing mass-based social movements of the kind that through the nineteenth and especially twentieth centuries, forced a resistant mainstream society to enact fundamental legislative reforms. Instead, younger donors, as well as many older ones, believe that exploiting educational and occupational opportunities is the best hope to ameliorate adverse community conditions and make structural changes. Moreover, education is seen as the key resource, whose acquisition by the community is transformative.

There is another element that is emerging, particularly among the younger donors: an appreciation of and an effort to build new networks within mainstream institutions and professions—not to tap into mainstream groups as token players but to build viable networks comprising people of color. A number of those we interviewed spoke of the privilege and power of holding important positions in the financial community. Their philanthropic dreams focused on replicating for others the conditions that allowed them to achieve their career goals. Education is seen as the vehicle, bright and talented young people of color are the instruments, and the objective is to build a critical mass within mainstream, often financial, institutions. The model is to train individuals and place them within strategic networks, not only to achieve affluence but also to accrue authority and influence that can be used to effect structural, social, and political change.

References

Anft, M., and Lipman, H. "How Americans Give." *Chronicle of Philanthropy*, May 1, 2003. [http://philanthropy.com/temp/email.php?id=xk3br6yh6r3 nxfwv2zbwvn1hv42z3656].

Carson, E. D. "Black Volunteers as Givers and Fundraisers." Working paper, Center for the Study of Philanthropy, 1990.

Chen, D. W. "Outer Suburbs Outpace City in Population Growth." *New York Times*, Mar. 16, 2001, p. B7.

Fields, A. B. *The Youth Challenge: Participating in Democracy.* New York: Carnegie Corporation of New York, 2003.

Gibson, C. *From Inspiration to Participation: A Review of Perspectives on Youth Civic Engagement.* Grantmaker Forum on Community and National Service, Nov. 2001. [http://www.pacefunders.org/publications/pubs/Moving%20Youth%20report%20REV3.pdf].

Giving USA. Glenview, Ill/: Giving USA Foundation, 2003.

INDEPENDENT SECTOR. 2001. *Giving and Volunteering in the United States.* Washington, D.C.: INDEPENDENT SECTOR, 2001.

New York City Housing and Vacancy Survey. 1991. Database.

New York City Housing and Vacancy Survey. 1999. Database.

Scott, J. "Boroughs' Rise Driven Largely by Immigration." *New York Times*, Mar. 16, 2001, pp. A1, B6.

U.S. Bureau of the Census. 1990. Database.

U.S. Bureau of the Census. 2000. Database.

FELINDA MOTTINO *and* EUGENE D. MILLER *are coproject directors of the Donor Research Project at the Center on Philanthropy and Civil Society, the Graduate Center, City University of New York.*

*Between now and 2055, the amount of wealth to
be transferred by African American households will
be small compared to the aggregate transfer from
all households. This relative scarcity places a special
emphasis on wise allocation of financial resources
and an equal burden on the organizations that
receive charitable donations to honor the gifts by
using them wisely.*

5

Wealth transfer estimates for African American households

John J. Havens, Paul G. Schervish

IN 2001 THERE WERE 13.2 million African American households in
the United States. These households constituted 12.4 percent of
all households, earned 7.1 percent of aggregate household income,
owned 2.5 percent of aggregate household wealth, and contributed
5.4 percent of aggregate household charitable giving.

This chapter summarizes selected findings from work in progress
at the Center on Wealth and Philanthropy at Boston College and

An expanded paper that includes additional findings, analysis, and a methodological
appendix is posted on our Web site, www.bc.edu/cwp. The Center on Wealth and Philanthropy (CWP) is grateful to the Twenty-First Century Foundation for sponsoring
the extension of wealth transfer estimates to African American households. CWP is
generously supported by the T. B. Murphy Foundation Charitable Trust and the Lilly
Endowment, whose funding supported the initial development of the wealth transfer
simulation model.

NEW DIRECTIONS FOR PHILANTHROPIC FUNDRAISING, NO. 48, SUMMER 2005 © WILEY PERIODICALS, INC.

presents new information on wealth and wealth transfer within the African American community.

Overview of findings

The trends in the financial resources (income and wealth) and philanthropy (cash and in-kind giving) of African American households are dialectical in that they portray two almost contradictory themes. The first theme is that income, wealth, and charitable giving in the African American community have risen rapidly in recent years. From 1992 through 2001, after adjustment for inflation, both aggregate income and aggregate wealth for African American households have risen at an annual rate of 4 percent, and aggregate charitable giving has risen at an annual rate of 5 percent. Part of the growth in these aggregates reflects an increase in the number of African American households, but the remaining part reflects changes in average income, wealth, and contributions per household. If we look only at the inflation-adjusted household averages for wealth, income, and charitable giving among African American households, we find the same pattern as shown by the aggregates, albeit at somewhat lower rates of growth. These income and wealth statistics demonstrate that African American households as a group gained substantial financial purchasing power in terms of both income and wealth during the period and that their charitable giving increased even faster than either their income or their wealth.

The second theme in these trends is that the share of aggregate national household income, aggregate national household wealth, and aggregate national household charitable giving in the African American community has declined during this same period. African American households increased their purchasing power during this period, but not as fast as non–African American households, especially non–African American households that own $1 million or more in net worth. In terms of aggregate financial resources, the African American community as a group was substantially better off in 2001 than in 1992, but their gains in income and wealth were not as large, on average, as for the total population, whose income and wealth grew even faster than that of African American households. As the financial resources of African American households grew, their charitable contributions more than kept pace with the rates of growth in income and wealth. Once again, however, the rate of growth in charitable contributions among non–African American households was even greater than among African American households, due in substantial part to the higher rates of growth in financial resources among non–African American households. The result is that African American households gave a larger amount but a smaller share of aggregate national household giving in 2001 than in 1992.

Wealth transfer microsimulation model

We used the Wealth Transfer Microsimulation Model (WTMM) developed and housed at the Center on Wealth and Philanthropy to estimate wealth transfer among African American households from 2001 through 2055. The model is based on data from the 2001 Survey of Consumer Finances, sponsored by the Board of Governors of the Federal Reserve System, mortality rates published by the National Center for Health Statistics, and historical patterns of the distribution of the value of final estates (estates without a surviving spouse) based on Internal Revenue Service (IRS) data on estate filings.

In each set of analyses, we developed estimates for three scenarios, defined in terms of secular growth. The low-growth scenario assumes a 2 percent national secular trend in the growth of wealth and a lower-than-average life cycle savings rates. The middle-growth scenario assumes a 3 percent national secular trend in growth of wealth and average life cycle savings rates. The high-growth scenario assumes a 4 percent national secular trend in the growth of wealth and higher than average life cycle savings rates.

The WTMM was used to produce estimates for each of these scenarios, assuming first that the high-growth rates among young African American households were a life cycle effect. It was then used to produce corresponding estimates for each of the three scenarios, assuming that the high-growth rates among young African American households were a cohort effect.

Distribution of wealth

Household wealth among African American households is unequally distributed both within the African American community and contrasted with non–African American households. There were relatively few (about 112,000) African American households that owned at least $1 million in wealth in 2001 and relatively few (about 333,000) that owned even $500,000 in 2001. This is important for the estimation of wealth transfer because (1) households must own wealth in order to transfer it, (2) the majority of wealth transfer for the population of all households originates in households whose estates are worth at least $1 million at the time of death, and (3) the fraction of the value of estates contributed to charity increases dramatically as the value of estates increase above $1 million. Because African American households own limited wealth compared with non–African American households, their potential for wealth transfer and charitable bequests is similarly limited.

Rate of growth in wealth

From 1992 through 2001, the inflation-adjusted rate of growth in the average wealth of African American households was about 2.42 percent as compared with 5.88 percent for all households during the same period. For any household, wealth grows from three sources: (1) net savings out of household income (household income less household taxes less household consumption), (2) appreciation of assets, and (3) net financial transfers (including forgiven debt and inheritance) to the household. On average, African American households have had lower amounts of savings, appreciation, and net transfers received as compared with non–African American households. Among other factors, one reason for these lower amounts is the concentration of African American households at the lower end of the income and wealth distributions. It is hard to accumulate much savings when household income is low. Appreciation of assets will not amount to much if you do not own many assets. If your parents and relatives were not themselves wealthy, it is unlikely you will receive much in the way of inheritance, and if you have succeeded nevertheless in doing fairly well financially, you may be transferring money out of the household to support your children and less fortunate relatives and friends. Finally, the more generous you are with your charitable contributions, the lower your net worth will be, at least in the short term.

The lower rate of growth in the wealth of African American households in relation to the rate of growth in wealth of all households is important to wealth transfer because the long-term rates of growth correspond to the secular rates of growth in our estimation of wealth transfer. The growth rate in the wealth for African American households is about half that for all households. If this relationship remains valid in the future, the 2 percent, 3 percent, and 4 percent rates of secular growth for all households imply 1 percent, 1.5 percent, and 2 percent corresponding rates of secular growth among African American households. These lower rates of secular growth further limit the amount of wealth that will be transferred from African American households.

However, our analysis reveals that the issue is somewhat more complex. We find that for the young age cohort (those age forty-one or younger), the rate of growth in wealth is slightly higher than the growth rate for all households in the same cohort and is the same as for Caucasian households in the same cohort. This is a striking finding, which raises the issue of whether this is a life cycle or a cohort effect. A life cycle effect means that African American households headed by someone in the young cohort enjoy high rates of growth in their wealth but that these rates drop as the head reaches middle and older age. A cohort effect means that African American households headed by someone in the young cohort enjoy high rates of growth in their wealth and continue to enjoy these high rates as the head continues to age. In our basic wealth transfer set of analyses, we assume that the high growth rate in the young African American cohort is a life cycle effect. We also ran an alternative set of analyses, however, in which we assume that it is a cohort effect. We find that the difference between corresponding estimates from the two sets of analyses is negligible for 2 percent secular rates of growth but becomes significant at 3 and 4 percent secular rates of growth, amounting to $0.4 trillion and $0.7 trillion in additional wealth transfer, respectively.

Estimates of wealth transfer

We measure the value of wealth transfer as the net worth of final estates at the death of the decedent. The major results of the simulation indicate that the total amount of wealth transfer from African American households will range from $1.1 trillion to $3.4 trillion (2003 dollars) during the fifty-five-year period from 2001 through 2055. The estimates ranged from $1.1 trillion (low-growth scenario) to $2.7 trillion (high-growth scenario) for the life cycle set of scenarios and from $1.2 trillion (low-growth scenario) to $3.4 trillion (high-growth scenario) for the cohort set of scenarios.

The estimates of wealth transfer from African American households are large, but they account for less than 2.5 percent of the $46.3 trillion to $153.7 trillion (2003 dollars) of our 1999 estimate of total wealth transfer for the nation. African American households constituted 12.4 percent of all households in 2001 but will generate less than 2.5 percent of the national total wealth transfer. This is due to the low endowment of wealth owned by African American households in 2001 and the lower-than-average rates of growth in the wealth of African American households.

The total amount of wealth transfer is not transferred in its entirety to heirs or to charitable causes. It is distributed among taxes, heirs, charitable bequests, and estate fees (including burial costs and legal fees). If wealth transferred from African American households follows national historical patterns, estate fees would range from $40 billion to $133 billion (2003 dollars), estate taxes would range from $71 billion to $687 billion (2003 dollars), charitable bequests would range from $40 billion to $283 billion (2003 dollars), and bequests to heirs would range from $939 billion to

$2.3 trillion (2003 dollars), depending on the scenario and assumption regarding life cycle versus cohort interpretation of high growth rates in wealth among young African American households.

According to our analysis, African American households will leave a greater fraction of their wealth to heirs and a smaller fraction to charity as compared with our national estimates of all households. African American households will bequeath from 68 to 87 percent of their wealth to heirs as compared with 48 to 60 percent bequeathed to heirs from all households. African American households will bequeath from 4 to 8 percent to charitable causes as compared with 15 to 18 percent bequeathed to charitable causes from all households.

In aggregate, African American households may appear less charitable than other households, but this is not true. The relatively low percentages bequeathed to charity by African American households reflect the concentration of African American estates below $1 million (and even below $500,000) and the relatively few African American estates that will be valued at $1 million or more. Historically, estates below $1 million bequeath relatively small proportions of their estates to charity (and relatively large proportions to heirs) in contrast to estates of $1 million or more, which bequeath relatively large proportions of their estates to charity (and relatively small proportions to heirs). The relatively higher concentration of African American estates at the lower end of the distribution of the value of estates means that African American households leave smaller percentages of their estates to charity (and higher percentages to heirs) compared with the percentage of the estates of all households left to charity (or to heirs).

Limitation of the estimates

The distribution of the value of estates to estate fees, charitable bequests, taxes, and heirs is based on national patterns for the entire population. At the current time, the data do not permit the examination of distributional patterns specific to African American households. If African American households depart from national patterns and leave larger or smaller fractions of their estates as charitable bequests as compared with non–African American households at the same level of wealth, their aggregate charitable bequests will be larger or smaller than the estimates in the scenario.

The WTMM model is based on trends in secular growth of household wealth; current mortality rates; distribution of estates among heirs, charity, taxes, and estate fees based on historical data from the IRS; and the joint distribution of wealth and demographic characteristics embedded in its microdata file. The WTMM uses the 2001 Survey of Consumer Finances (SCF) as its microdata file, which is a subset of data from the 2001 SCF. The SCF has no over-sample of African American households. It contains 462 African American households in the sample; only 21 of these households have assets in excess of $500,000, and 12 have assets in excess of $1 million. The sample is thus sparse at the high end of assets and wealth. The degree to which the sample is nonrepresentative of the high-wealth African American population is an important open question. To the extent that this group is underrepresented, the wealth transfer estimates are conservatively low.

Implications of wealth transfer for wealth and charitable bequests

Because African Americans on average have proportionately lower values of household wealth and also lower-than-average growth rates in wealth, relatively small percentages of the total value of African American final estates (29 to 63 percent) will be concentrated in a very small number (1.3 to 6.0 percent) of African American households, whose final estates will have a net worth of $1 million or more. These households will account for a lower-than-average proportion (61 to 87 percent) of charitable bequests.

The implication for fundraising among African American households is that such efforts may have to follow strategies that differ from fundraising among households in general. Although successful strategies may involve extending efforts to lower levels of affluence, strategies may more likely be successful if they engage affluent and wealthy African Americans in a process of discernment to identify and act on their own values and goals with respect to their philanthropy.

In addition to intensifying the fundraising efforts that are already in place in communities and churches, this analysis suggests three strategies for increasing charitable giving among African American households. The first is to work more directly and intensely with the relatively few identifiable very high-wealth African American households populated by celebrities, athletes, and business owners in order to create a more visible culture of giving that will set the tone for and inspire giving among their peers and others. The second is to develop a longer-term strategy for the cohort of young African American professionals and business owners who may not at this time be very wealthy but will become very wealthy as their assets grow over the next two decades, perhaps at rates comparable to their white counterparts. The third strategy is the most obvious mainly because it is so fundamentally true. The most consequential long-term strategy for increasing African American philanthropy is to increase African American income and wealth. This means bolstering educational attainment, business ownership, and home ownership. The greater the income and wealth of households, including African American ones, the more is given to philanthropy, both in inter vivos giving and through charitable bequests. In the end, perhaps the most creative and effective strategy might be to enlist the philanthropy of the identifiable celebrities, athletes, and business owners to accomplish the third strategy.

JOHN J. HAVENS *is associate director and senior research associate at the Center on Wealth and Philanthropy, Boston College.*

PAUL G. SCHERVISH *is director at the Center on Wealth and Philanthropy and professor, Department of Sociology, Boston College.*

New data help to determine whether differences in philanthropic practices are due to race and ethnicity themselves or to a variety of factors that are correlated with these labels.

6

Religious and secular giving, by race and ethnicity

Richard Steinberg, Mark Wilhelm

PATTERNS OF GIVING and volunteering by different racial and ethnic groups have been subjected to increasingly sophisticated scrutiny of late. Surveys (for example, Hodgkinson and Weitzman, 1996) suggest that African American and Hispanic families are less likely to make charitable donations or volunteer and make smaller average donations (or volunteer fewer hours) than white and Anglo families. However, the interpretation of these results is far from clear for at least four reasons. First, differences in giving and volunteering may result from differences in income, education, and other factors rather than race or ethnicity. Second, differences may reflect differing selective response rates. Those who are less generous may not admit this to the interviewer, and the willingness to answer questions may differ across racial or ethnic groups. Third, differences may reflect patterns of charitable solicitation or volunteer recruitment rather than differences in underlying generosity. Finally, differences in reported giving and volunteering may reflect

This chapter was prepared with the assistance of Heidi Baker.

NEW DIRECTIONS FOR PHILANTHROPIC FUNDRAISING, NO. 48, SUMMER 2005 © WILEY PERIODICALS, INC.

differing understandings of the survey questions rather than differences in real behavior.

Our study contributes to the first two aspects of interpretation. We employ a large and rich data source, the Center on Philanthropy Panel Study (COPPS), to determine whether racial and ethnic differences remain after the confounding effects of other factors are removed. COPPS data are of extremely high quality, with exceptional response rates to questions about giving (Wilhelm, 2003). COPPS began in 2001 as a supplement attached to the Panel Study on Income Dynamics (PSID), an ongoing survey repeated annually from 1968 to 1999 and every two years since then. The PSID has followed the same individuals since its inception, together with their progeny and anyone else who became part of their (or their children's) families. For the 2001 wave analyzed here, there are 7,406 PSID family units, almost all of whom responded to the COPPS questions. From the rest of the PSID, we have an extensive and carefully constructed set of control variables with which to conduct our analysis.

What do other studies find?

Studies that control for confounding factors come to diverse conclusions about whether apparent differences in giving or volunteering are due to race or ethnicity. Carson (1989) finds that blacks are substantially less likely to make charitable donations than whites at every level of income, his only control variable. Conley (2000) notes the distinction between income (the rate at which financial resources are arriving) and wealth (the total financial resources available at a point in time), criticizing Carson for his failure to include the latter. Using PSID data from 1994, he finds that blacks have substantially lower wealth at all levels of income than whites. Furthermore, he finds that other control variables commonly used in studies of racial differences in giving do not serve as adequate proxies for the missing data on wealth.

He speculates that wealth controls would eliminate the remaining difference in giving but bemoans the lack of appropriate data, recommending that "a new survey be conducted that combines aspects of the PSID and the Joint Center-Gallup Survey of Philanthropic Activity" (p. 538). That is precisely what COPPS does, and we report the results here.

O'Neill and Roberts (2000) report on a survey of about thirty-six hundred California residents interviewed in 1998–1999. They find that white, African American, and Asian/Pacific Islanders give and volunteer at comparable rates and levels, whereas Latinos have lower participation rates. These differences disappear when results are adjusted for differences in income, education, and immigration status.

Eschholz and Van Slyke (2002) find a mixed pattern for blacks in the metropolitan Atlanta area. They find that blacks are significantly less likely to make a donation after controlling for age, education, marital status, employment, children in the household, religious service attendance, political party, gender, and attitude toward government. Race has no effect on the amount given in general, but among women, blacks gave significantly less than whites. Finally, there are no significant differences in the likelihoods of black and white volunteering. Notably, they could not control for income because 47 percent of respondents refused to answer the question. In a related paper, Van Slyke and Eschholz (2002) find that blacks volunteer more than whites, with the difference significant for black women but not men. Interestingly, they find that men in the category Other Race volunteer significantly less than either black or white men.

Yen (2002) employs data from the 1995 Consumer Expenditure Survey. He too finds that race effects disappear from a system of equations that explain charity, religious, and other organizational giving once one controls for income, age, and education. Musick, Wilson, and Bynum (2000) cite six previous studies that find that racial differences in volunteering disappear once controls for socioeconomic status are included, two that find that whites volunteer more than blacks even after controls, one that finds white women are more likely to volunteer than black women but volunteer the same number of hours when they do, and four that find blacks volunteering more than whites. They attribute the differences to varying definitions of volunteering, methods of analysis, and subject populations and call for more study with better data sets. Their own study finds the gap reduced but still present after introducing a variety of control variables, with blacks volunteering less than whites.

Mesch, Rooney, Chin, and Steinberg (2004) analyze the giving and volunteering of 885 Indiana respondents. They find that race does not affect the probability of making a donation, the size of the gift, the probability of volunteering, or the amount of volunteering after controlling for gender, marital status, income, age, education, and survey methodology. A follow-up study (Rooney, Mesch, Chin, and Steinberg, forthcoming) obtained similar results for the probability of donating and the size of the gift using a national sample of forty-two hundred respondents.

In summary, existing literature is not voluminous and obtains mixed results on whether racial and ethnic differences are real. Existing studies are hampered by potentially serious omitted-variable bias, particularly that caused by the omission of family wealth. Existing studies also suffer, to an unknown degree, from biases due to nonresponse to survey questions on giving and volunteering.

Monetary gifts, by race of family head

Our main findings report on donations by African American families (those whose head is African American regardless of the race of other members of the family unit) versus donations by other families (whom we refer to as white in this chapter). These results indicate that if we remove the confounding influences of other variables, there is no significant difference between the giving of black and white families. If anything, black families are slightly more generous ($1,363 per family versus $1,325). Blacks are noticeably more generous in religious giving ($924 versus $814) and a bit less generous in secular giving ($439 versus $510), although these differences are not statistically significant.

Our method for computing this is a bit nonstandard and needs further explanation. First, we use multivariate methods to estimate an equation that can be used to predict the giving of anyone in the sample from knowledge of their income, education, wealth, race, ethnicity, and many other factors. (We also included controls for generation, sex, marital status, number and age of children, health status, region, city size, and religious denomination. For further details, a longer version of this chapter is available from us.) Using this equation, we obtain the predicted giving of every black family in the sample. For white families, we predict how much they would give if their income, education, wealth, and other variables remained the same, but instead of being headed by a white, they were headed by a black. Combining these two sets of predictions, we compute average donations if every family in the sample was black. Then we repeat the exercise, this time leaving the white families alone and predicting the giving of black families if they were to "turn white." The difference between these two numbers is our estimate of the impact of race.

Monetary gifts, by ethnicity of family head

The analysis for ethnicity reveals that apparent differences between Hispanics and others are due to the other factors rather than ethnicity. We predict that if everyone in the sample were Hispanic but retained current levels of income and other factors, that average gifts per family would be $1,195 versus $1,336 for non-Hispanic families and $1,251 for families whose ethnicity is not known to us. These differences are quite noticeable, but not large enough to provide assurance that they represent something real rather than the luck of the draw in constructing our sample; in technical terms, the differences are not statistically significant.

Volunteering, by race of family head

Unlike donations, which are reported at the family level, volunteering is reported at the individual level for family heads and family wives/"wives." Under PSID nomenclature, adult women or men are regarded as family heads if no spouse or long-term cohabitant of the opposite sex is present, regardless of their marital status. If a spouse or long-term cohabitant of the opposite sex from the head is present, this person is regarded as the wife or "wife" regardless of gender and marital status. The term *Wife/"Wife"* is awkward, and we shall henceforth refer to this person as the spouse. Thus, we report our findings separately for (1) heads where no spouse is present, (2) heads where a spouse is present, (3) spouses, and (4) families where both a head and spouse are present.

Data on volunteering by heads when no spouse is present strongly suggest that black single heads are less likely to volunteer, but despite this fact, the average number of hours volunteered (including nonvolunteers in the computation of the average) is about the same as that for whites. Our results suggest 15 percent of black single heads volunteer a predicted average of thirty-nine hours versus 26 percent of white single heads volunteering a predicted average of thirty-eight hours. This is due to the fact that blacks who do volunteer give many more hours on average than white volunteers do. We note that there are only thirty-three volunteers who are single black heads in our sample, so this average is strongly affected by a few outliers who may or may not be representative of the broader population. We then report adjusted estimates that take account of the fact that our black volunteers differ in many ways other than race from white volunteers. Our adjustments here are far more tentative than those we provide for donations due to the press of time, and although we find that predicted average volunteering by single black heads is about an hour more than that for single white heads, this difference is not statistically significant.

The pattern is different for black heads with spouses present. Blacks are less likely to volunteer but give more hours when they do volunteer, so that there is no apparent difference in the predicted average hours, including nonvolunteers.

The pattern for spouses is very similar to the pattern for heads in families where both are present. Spouses of black heads are substantially less likely to volunteer (18 percent versus 34 percent) and volunteer substantially fewer hours, regardless of the exclusion of nonvolunteers. There is a bit more precision about our preliminary estimates of predicted average volunteering: twenty-four hours for blacks versus forty-five for whites, statistically significant at the 11 percent level.

Finally, we present our data for family volunteering (the sum of head and spouse volunteering). Once again, blacks appear to volunteer less in every way this is measured. Our preliminary estimates of predicted average volunteering are the clearest yet, showing forty-six hours for black families versus eighty hours for white families, a difference that is statistically significant at the 10 percent level. However, his figures for predicted volunteering are preliminary.

Conclusion

In this chapter, we advance the literature on whether apparent differences in the giving and volunteering of black versus white, or Hispanic versus other families, are real. We employ new data, COPPS, that allow us to determine whether the differences are due to race and ethnicity themselves or a variety of factors that are correlated with these labels. Otherwise identical black and white families vary in many ways not captured by other available studies, especially in their stock of available assets—their net wealth. We control for family wealth. Our data have much lower levels of nonresponse than other available data, so we also gather evidence on whether apparent differences are due to differential response rates to surveys.

We find that differences in giving are indeed an artifact of confounding variables. We estimate that if everyone's race or ethnicity changed but their income, wealth, education, and many other factors remained the same, the average family donations would not change very much; we cannot reject the hypothesis that race and ethnicity have no effect whatsoever on total family giving. There are some hints that otherwise identical blacks give a larger share of their donations to religious causes, but this difference is not statistically significant. The picture is more complicated if our estimates for volunteering are taken at face value, but these estimates are quite preliminary. Single-headed black families are predicted to volunteer about the same amount as single-headed white families, but both black family heads and their spouses volunteer substantially less than their white counterparts in families where both are present, so that total volunteering is significantly lower in black families.

To place these results in context, let us recall the other problems suffered by studies of this type. We are unable to deal with the third and fourth problems cited in the introduction: differential solicitation and volunteer recruitment and differential understanding of survey questions. Wilson and Musick (1997, 1998) and Musick, Wilson, and Bynum (2000) find that patterns of volunteer recruitment matter; Bryant, Jeon-Slaughter, Kang, and Tax (2003) extend these results to solicitation of money. The latter find, however, that even controlling for solicitation status, blacks (and, less significantly, Hispanics) are less likely to volunteer and donate.

Differences in reported giving and volunteering may also reflect differing understandings of the survey questions rather than differences in real behavior. For example, Smith, Shue, Vest, and Villarreal (1999) find that some ethnic groups describe their philanthropic activities as "'sharing' and 'helping'" (p. 6) rather than "charity." These groups may not recall or report the full extent of their queried activities in response to memory prompts and questions that speak of donations to nonprofit organizations. Some aspects are explored in a series of papers that look at differences in reported giving and volunteering by type of questionnaire (Rooney, Steinberg, and Schervish, 2001; Steinberg, Rooney, and Chin, 2002; Rooney, Steinberg, and Schervish, 2004), and whether the type of questionnaire matters in the same way to respondents of different races or genders (Mesch, Rooney, Chin, and Steinberg, 2004; Rooney, Mesch, Chin, and Steinberg, forthcoming).

If the differences are real, there are still questions about whether they are meaningful. Carson (1991) points out that if the causes typically supported by blacks (and, by extension, Hispanics) have different needs, there is no reason to expect black supporters to have the same generosity exhibited by supporters of other causes. In addition, generosity is expressed in many ways other than formal giving and volunteering through nonprofit organizations, including immigrant remittances, help to family and friends, gifts to strangers, and even donation of blood and body parts. Do differences found in, say, volunteering reflect differences in the level of generosity, or merely its composition? A bit of evidence on this comes from Carson (1989), who finds that blacks are more likely to give money, food or clothing, or perform some other service for the homeless or for a needy friend at all surveyed levels of income, and for a needy neighbor, a needy relative, or a needy individual at some levels of income.

References

Bryant, W. K., Jeon-Slaughter, H., Kang, H., and Tax, A. "Participation in Philanthropic Activities: Donating Money and Time." *Journal of Consumer Policy*, 2003, *26*, 42–73.

Carson, E. D. "The Evolution of Black Philanthropy: Patterns of Giving and Voluntarism." In R. Magat (ed.), *Philanthropic Giving: Studies in Varieties and Goals*. New York: Oxford University Press, 1989.

Carson, E. D. "Contemporary Trends in Black Philanthropy: Challenging the Myths." In D. F. Burlingame and L. J. Hulse (eds.), *Taking Fund Raising Seriously: Advancing the Profession and Practice of Raising Money*. San Francisco: Jossey-Bass, 1991.

Conley, D. "The Racial Wealth Gap: Origins and Implications for Philanthropy in the African American Community." *Nonprofit and Voluntary Sector Quarterly*, 2000, *29*, 530–540.

Eschholz, S. L., and Van Slyke, D. M. "New Evidence About Women and Philanthropy: Findings from Metro Atlanta." Mimeographed, Georgia State University, 2002.

Hodgkinson, V. A., and Weitzman, M. *Giving and Volunteering in the United States: Findings from a National Survey*. Washington, D.C.: INDEPENDENT SECTOR, 1996.

Mesch, D. J., Rooney, P. M., Chin, W., and Steinberg, K. S. "The Effects of Race, Gender, and Measurement on Giving and Volunteering: Indiana as a Test Case." Working paper, Center on Philanthropy at Indiana University, 2004.

Musick, M. A., Wilson, J., and Bynum, W. B. "Race and Formal Volunteering: The Differential Effects of Call and Religion." *Social Forces*, 2000, *78*, 1539–1571.

O'Neill, M., and Roberts, W. *Giving and Volunteering in California*. San Francisco: University of San Francisco, Institute for Nonprofit Organization Management, 2000.

Rooney, P. M., Mesch, D. J., Chin, W., and Steinberg, K. S. "The Effects of Race, Gender, and Survey Methodologies on Giving in the U.S." *Economics Letters*, forthcoming.

Rooney, P. M., Steinberg, K. S., and Schervish, P. G. "A Methodological Comparison of Giving Surveys: Indiana as a Test Case." *Nonprofit and Voluntary Sector Quarterly*, 2001, *30*, 551–568.

Rooney, P. M., Steinberg, K. S., and Schervish, P. G. "Methodology Is Destiny." *Nonprofit and Voluntary Sector Quarterly*, 2004, *33*, 628–654.

Smith, B., Shue, S., Vest, J. L., and Villarreal, J. *Philanthropy in Communities of Color*. Bloomington: Indiana University Press, 1999.

Steinberg, K. S., Rooney, P. M., and Chin, W. "Measurement of Volunteering: A Methodological Study Using Indiana as a Test Case." *Nonprofit and Voluntary Sector Quarterly*, 2002, *31*, 484–501.

Van Slyke, D. M., and Eschholz, S. L. "Are Women More Generous than Men? Gender Differences in Motivations for Charitable Giving." Paper presented at the ARNOVA Annual Conference, Montreal, Quebec, Canada, 2002.

Wilhelm, M. "The Distribution of Giving in Six Surveys." Mimeographed, Indiana University–Purdue University Indianapolis, 2003.

Wilson, J., and Musick, M. A. "Who Cares? Toward an Integrated Theory of Volunteer Work." *American Sociological Review*, 1997, *62*, 694–713.

Wilson, J., and Musick, M. A. "The Contribution of Social Resources to Volunteering." *Social Science Quarterly*, 1998, *79*, 799–814.

Yen, S. T. "An Econometric Analysis of Household Donations in the USA." *Applied Economics Letters*, 2002, *9*, 837–841.

RICHARD STEINBERG *is professor of economics, philanthropic studies, and public affairs, Indiana University–Purdue University Indianapolis, and associate director of the Center on Philanthropy Panel Study.*

MARK WILHELM *is associate professor of economics and philanthropic studies, Indiana University–Purdue University Indianapolis, and director of the Center on Philanthropy Panel Study.*

*What do the new provisions for Charitable Choice
mean for faith-based African American charitable
organizations?*

7

Government shekels and government
shackles revisited: Questions for
church and state

Sheila Suess Kennedy

IN 1996, CONGRESS PASSED the Personal Responsibility and Work
Opportunity Reconciliation Act, reforming welfare "as we know
it." Among its provisions was a section called "Charitable Choice,"
requiring states to contract with faith-based social service providers
on the same basis as they contract with other nonprofits. The bill
specified that "pervasively sectarian" organizations were not to be
discriminated against, that such providers should be allowed to
maintain hiring policies based on their religious dictates, and that
they could not be required to divest the premises where services
were delivered of religious iconography. Charitable Choice provisions were subsequently added to other legislation and eventually
became the template for President George W. Bush's "faith-based
initiative."

Government had partnered with religious organizations and their
affiliates for decades; nevertheless, Charitable Choice was immedi-
ately attacked from both left and right. Civil libertarians objected
to provisions that allowed religious providers to discriminate in

NEW DIRECTIONS FOR PHILANTHROPIC FUNDRAISING, NO. 48, SUMMER 2005 © WILEY PERIODICALS, INC.

employment. Religious right activists demanded assurances that funds would not go to disfavored groups like the Nation of Islam. African American pastors in urban areas, arguably the main targets of the initiative, expressed concern that "government shekels" would be accompanied by "government shackles"—that the costs and regulatory burdens that accompany collaborations with government would divert resources from client services and, even more troubling, would mute the church's historic prophetic voice (Kennedy and Bielefeld, 2001).

Background and context

Government agencies have provided services through nonprofit and religious organizations since the inception of government social welfare programs, although characterization of Charitable Choice and President Bush's faith-based initiative as "new" or even "revolutionary" has tended to obscure that history (U.S. Senate Judiciary Committee, 2001). One of the difficulties faced by analysts of these measures is that neither the legislation nor the White House Office of Faith-Based and Community Initiatives has explained what is new about these efforts or has defined what *faith based* means for purposes of Charitable Choice, leaving researchers to wonder what precisely is new.

Many religious providers with long-standing histories of social welfare provision are faith based in the most literal sense—that is, the provision of essentially secular social services is motivated by their religious beliefs. Feeding and clothing the poor, tending the sick, and housing the aged are approached as religious duties rather than as opportunities for proselytizing or transforming the individuals served. However, this is by no means universally true of religious organizations that have historically received government funding (Task Force on Sectarian Social Services and Public Funding, 1990). The Salvation Army has long received substantial funding, despite being "pervasively sectarian" by almost any definition of that term (Winston, 2001). Congregations are faith based by definition, yet studies show that 20 percent of congregations that provide social services collaborated with government agencies before passage of Charitable Choice (U.S. Senate Judiciary Committee, 2001; M. Chaves, interview by the author, 2001).

Given this history, it would have been helpful had Congress addressed several important questions: What does *faith based* mean for purposes of Charitable Choice legislation and the faith-based initiative? Do faith-based organizations targeted by the Charitable Choice legislation differ from those with a long history of governmental contractual relationships? If so, how? What are the barriers to their participation in social service delivery that this effort proposes to eliminate? To what extent are those barriers practically necessary or constitutionally required? What are the availability and interest and what are the capacities of these organizations? Few of these questions found their way into the congressional debates about Charitable Choice (Kennedy, 2003), and none were addressed by the legislation.

Charitable Choice legislation was explicitly predicated on the assumption that faith-based organizations were more effective at providing assistance than the secular and religiously affiliated nonprofits that had delivered the bulk of tax-supported social welfare programs on government's behalf. However, there were no empirical data available either to support or rebut that presumption. In September 2000, with support from the Ford Foundation, our research team sought to answer that question, among others; we began work on a three-year evaluation of Charitable Choice implementation by three states: Indiana, Massachusetts, and North Carolina. (The results of that research are available at http://ccr.urbancenter.iupui.edu, and will be the subject of a forthcoming book.)

One of the products of our research was a video for use by government agencies and congregations considering a new faith-based partnership. In it, we identified three significant sets of questions that prospective partners should be prepared to answer in order to decide if the proposed collaboration is likely to be mutually beneficial.

The three C's of Charitable Choice

In the course of our research, we interviewed dozens of people in the religious community: agency directors, faith leaders, and constitutional experts who have managed and studied effective partnerships, as well as those that have failed. Those interviews suggest three areas for careful consideration: capacity, commitment, and constitutionality. By capacity, we mean an evaluation of the assets each partner brings to the collaboration: personnel, money, expertise, and facilities. By commitment, we mean willingness based on a clear understanding of what the partnership entails and the responsibilities the partners are assuming. And by constitutionality, we mean affirmative answers to two important questions: Do both partners understand what the law requires, and are they prepared to abide by those requirements?

Capacity

Assessing capacity requires calculating how many people will be required to manage and staff the proposed program and whether those persons will be paid staff, volunteers, or a combination. Research suggests that congregations tend to be most successful with programs that are short term and finite: it is one thing to collect food for a food pantry and quite another to run a daily meals program. The average congregation has seventy-five people; the average annual congregational budget is $100,000 (M. J. Bane, interview with N. Hiatt, 2002). If an average congregation is proposing to enter a contract to provide social services, it is likely that those services will depend heavily on volunteers. How dependable will those volunteers be during sustained program periods? Will they be diverted from other congregational tasks? If so, who will take over those jobs? Do the volunteers have the experience and background necessary to provide the services in question? If the congregation is counting heavily on a particular volunteer, does it have a plan for what would happen if she falls ill or moves or dies? Does it have a backup?

The personnel challenge was summed up by Reverend Odell Cleveland, who runs the very successful Welfare Reform Liaison Project in North Carolina:

When you talk about replicating a program, you have to have compassion and expertise. Ninety-seven percent of my staff have degrees; some of them advanced degrees. It's more than sister so-and-so who's willing to help. People have to be trained. People have to be educated and trained and know what they're dealing with, because you can have all the good intentions in the world, but if you are not trained and qualified to handle these situations, if you're not careful, you can do more harm than good [interview with N. Hiatt, 2002].

Capacity also includes financial considerations. How will this program be funded? Will all the money come from the government? If so, what will happen if the contract is not renewed? What about cash flow? In many states, payment is made only when a desired outcome has occurred: when the client is placed in a job, or leaves welfare, or achieves whatever the program's goal may be. If services must be provided for several months before payment is received, can the congregation finance services during that time?

Transaction costs are an often overlooked capacity issue and can come as a shock to small programs that previously did not have to cope with the accounting and paperwork demands of government agencies. These are not arbitrary or unwarranted requirements; if a government agency is committing tax dollars to a program, it has an obligation to ensure that the money is being properly spent. However, that entails periodic audits, site visits, and paperwork that most congregations have not previously encountered. Does the congregation have the accountants, bookkeepers, and clerical support needed to comply? Have the costs of compliance been factored into the contract amount? Will resources have to be diverted from client service to compliance?

The final capacity question concerns program size. Will the contract require an expansion of services? If so, is the expansion feasible? Some social scientists have suggested that the virtue of many grassroots religious programs—the reason programs are success-ful—is their small scale and ability to engage clients personally. If the program must grow in order to comply with the government contract, will it lose the immediacy that made it work?

Commitment

The primary mission of a congregation is ministry. Before a congregation contracts to provide social services, it needs to consider whether the contract will divert attention and resources from that primary mission. A corollary question is whether contracting with government will mute the congregation's prophetic voice. As the Reverend John Buehrens of the Unitarian Universalist Association warns, "If you're on the government dole, your independence as a servant of God who is called to comfort the afflicted, yes, but also to afflict the comfortable and also to speak the moral word to government, becomes diminished. That's a great danger. It's a spiritual danger" (interview with N. Hiatt, 2002).

There are practical questions as well. If a preschool program is noisy and the children are rambunctious, will members of the congregation be annoyed? If the meals program increases wear and tear on the church kitchen, will congregants balk at the expense of maintenance and repair? If the program serves people very different from those in the congregation—poorer people, those from different racial and ethnic backgrounds, immigrants, former convicts—will the congregation still support the program?

Commitment can be evaluated by asking these questions: What is the congregation's goal? Is it congruent with government's goal? Is the congregation prepared for the inconvenience and disruption that may accompany the program? And perhaps most important, are the expectations on both sides of the partnership, governmental and congregational, clear?

Constitutional constraints

Questions of capacity and commitment apply to all proposed government contractors, secular or faith based. But the First Amendment creates added issues for religious contractors. Congregations considering a government contract must be prepared to live within the constitutional rules, whether or not it agrees with them.

The First Amendment prohibits the use of tax dollars to support religious organizations or for religious purposes; however, what constitutes support or a religious purpose is often unclear. The U.S. Supreme Court has never ruled that government may not purchase secular goods or services from religious entities, and to take such a position would raise serious equal protection and free exercise concerns. Historically, however, the Court has refused to allow the flow of direct government aid (as opposed to vouchers) to organizations that are "pervasively sectarian," that is, organizations whose religious character so permeates their service delivery as to make it impossible to divorce sacred from secular. Congregations, by definition, are pervasively sectarian.

In an effort to determine whether congregational leaders know the rules that govern faith-based partnerships, we surveyed congregations in South Bend, Indiana. (South Bend is large and diverse enough to be representative but small enough to be manageable. It is the fourth-largest city in Indiana, with a population of approximately 108,000. It is part of an eleven-county metropolitan area known as Michiana, which has nearly 1 million residents and 357,000 households.) We constructed a simple instrument, testing for very basic constitutional principles.

The results supported one clear conclusion: congregational leaders do not know what they need to know if they are to do business with government. Of 103 responses, 75 disagreed with the statement "The First Amendment and other provisions of the Bill of Rights apply only to government action." Understanding that the Bill of Rights limits only government action is basic to understanding the operation of American constitutional principles. Worse, 70 respondents disagreed with the statement, "If a congregation has a contract with government to provide services, the congregation may not include religious instruction or prayer as part of the services funded under the contract." Forty-nine respondents (almost half) disagreed with the statement, "The First Amendment's separation of church and state means that tax dollars cannot be used to fund religion or religious expression." In addition to a wrong response, several respondents wrote marginal notes to the effect that separation of church and state is not constitutionally required and that they would feel no compunction using tax dollars to save souls.

It bears emphasizing that there is no constitutional reason that congregations cannot partner with government; the issue is how such partnerships are conducted. Existing law is very clear about some things: government can buy food for the needy from a congregation, but the congregation cannot require recipients to pray before eating it. Government can rent beds in a faith-based homeless shelter, but use of those beds cannot be conditional on attendance at Bible study. Congregations need not take the crucifix off the wall or hide the Bibles, but they cannot use tax dollars to purchase those or other religious items. Failure to understand these rules (or unwillingness to abide by them) is a danger signal for any government partnership.

Conclusion

Before a congregation signs on the dotted line, there should be full communication with the government partner and with those in the congregation who will become stakeholders in the partnership. Becoming a government contractor may be right for a particular organization, or not. If there has been full discussion and due consideration of the pros and cons—if the congregation has the capacity to perform, the commitment to stay the course, and the knowledge and willingness to abide by the U.S. Constitution—the chances for a successful collaboration are good.

References

Kennedy, S. S. "Privatization and Prayer: The Case of Charitable Choice." *American Review of Public Administration*, 2003, *33*(1), 5–19.

Kennedy, S. S., and Bielefeld, W. "Government Shekels or Government Shackles: The Administrative Challenges of Charitable Choice." *Public Administration Review*, 2001, *62*(1).

Task Force on Sectarian Social Services and Public Funding. "Report of the Task Force on Sectarian Social Services." New York: American Jewish Committee, 1990.

U.S. Senate Judiciary Committee. *Faith Based Solutions: What Are the Legal Issues? Hearing Before the Judiciary Committee.* 107th Cong., 1st sess., June 6, 2001.

Winston, D. "Losing Their Religion?" 2001. [http://www.killingthebuddha.com/damn_nation/losing_their_religion.htm].

SHEILA SUESS KENNEDY *is associate professor in the School of Public and Environmental Affairs, Indiana University–Purdue University Indianapolis.*

The concept of black philanthropy should be expanded to include practices derived from African diasporan cultural traditions that have had both historical and contemporary influences on American philanthropy.

8

Promoting diversity in contemporary black philanthropy: Toward a new conceptual model

Jacqueline Copeland-Carson

THE TERM *BLACK PHILANTHROPY* as it is generally used refers to the giving traditions mostly of African Americans who were born in the United States. Increasingly, particularly with the increased immigration of people of African descent from Africa, the Caribbean, and Latin America to the United States, this focus is insufficient to understand philanthropy in a global economy. This chapter provides an overview of key, shared features of black American philanthropy as well as diverse practice being introduced by today's African immigrants. Unfortunately, there are very few studies of either African or black philanthropy in a diasporan context. Thus, the observations here should be seen as suggestive of areas for future research, not as definitive conclusions or prescriptions for action.

The views in this chapter do not necessarily reflect the opinions or positions of U.S. Bancorp or the University of Minnesota, or any of their subsidiaries, divisions, or employees.

NEW DIRECTIONS FOR PHILANTHROPIC FUNDRAISING, NO. 48, SUMMER 2005 © WILEY PERIODICALS, INC.

Black philanthropy in the United States, as well as black American culture in general, has always developed within a global context with cultural influences from various parts of Africa as well as the Caribbean and Europe (J. E. Harris, 1982; Thornton, 1992; Walters, 1993; Jalloh and Maizlish, 1996; Hine and McLeod, 1999; Vickerman, 1999; Yelvington, 2001). Black philanthropy can be more fully understood in the context of the intercontinental dynamics that also helped to shape it. The lack of a conceptual model that encompasses the full cultural diversity of black philanthropy in the United States impedes our ability to fully develop and maximize the potential of this resource to address shared community concerns.

Indigenous African philanthropy

The first theoretical hurdle that must be crossed to create a more inclusive model of black philanthropy in the United States is to define those activities that would be considered philanthropic across the multiple societies and groups that comprise the continent's diaspora. Philanthropy is not limited to formal charitable institutions or developed nations. It also includes informal social networks, practices, and traditions that foster mutual aid and reciprocity that have existed throughout history in all societies among people of varying financial means. From this perspective, philanthropy, including practices in the African diaspora, consists of the voluntary means that any culture or social group uses to redistribute financial and other resources for the purposes of promoting the collective good. The institutional mechanisms and social obligations that surround these voluntary practices will vary across societies and their constituent communities and may not be explicitly defined as philanthropic from a conventional Western perspective.

Africans have traditionally had a wide variety of philanthropic practices that were adapted by African Americans in the colonial period and continue to influence the sector through the practices of contemporary immigrants. Although the formal research on indigenous African philanthropy and its history is limited, a general sense of indigenous African philanthropy before the transatlantic slave trade and European colonialism can be gained from historical and anthropological research on other aspects of African life during these historical periods (see Feierman, 1998, for one of the few scholarly studies of precolonial African philanthropy). This is an important first step in understanding diasporan philanthropy because many of the practices that emerge, for example, in colonial America, could be adaptations of traditions established before formal European rule in Africa. Although a presentation of the history of indigenous African philanthropy is beyond the scope of this chapter (see Copeland-Carson, 2003), focusing on West and Central Africa, I highlight some key features and how they may have influenced early black philanthropy in the United States.

In addition to the extended family, there are a variety of indigenous social institutions that served philanthropic purposes in precolonial West and Central Africa. For example, there was a complex set of voluntary associations that included persons who were not necessarily relatives. Often organized around a common age cohort, occupation, or gender, these associations provided an important means for creating social networks beyond one's kin group. Association members provided support in times of trouble, and members could pool resources for a variety of social or political projects. These were sometimes secret societies that specialized in a particular ritual or spiritual knowledge or had some function in either maintaining or challenging the established social order (see, for example, Butt-Thompson, 1969; Boone, 1986).

Many of these voluntary groups operated revolving community funds. Called by a variety of names throughout Africa, these funds often provided an alternative to kin-based assistance, although a kin group could establish a fund. For example, members of a Yoruba women's craft guild would contribute a set amount of resources on a weekly, monthly, or annual basis, and each participating member would have a turn to use the entire pool for economic or social projects on a rotating basis. Called an *esusu* or *isu*, these indigenous financing tools provided an important source of support that could be used for a variety of collective purposes, including community social projects, political efforts, or the economic betterment of individual members and their families. These revolving community funds, ubiquitous in precolonial Africa, can be seen as indigenous foundations and are at least a partial basis for some of the contemporary philanthropy we see throughout the African diaspora in the Americas (Bascom, 1952; Siebel, 2000).[1] Their added value was increasing the capital access of individual members and allowing support of larger-scale community projects through the structured pooling of individual resources. These revolving funds were arguably philanthropic because they pooled participants' resources not only to support their individual interests but also often to support collective community needs.

Although a description of the philanthropic role of religious institutions in philanthropy is also beyond the scope of this chapter, these organizations played an important role in the redistribution of resources for charitable purposes in precolonial Africa (for examples, see Iliffe, 1987; Feierman, 1998).

The African roots of black philanthropy in America

Philanthropy among American blacks did not develop in a cultural vacuum. Although victimized by slavery, African peoples transplanted many of their social practices, including indigenous approaches to philanthropy, to the Americas. Americans of African descent adapted their imported ancestral traditions to create new philanthropic practices—part of a distinctly African diasporan approach to giving and voluntary assistance in the New World that has continued to evolve. Within the Americas, distinct streams of African diasporan philanthropy developed that shared many features in common but also had regional differences based on the particular community and national histories.

Most of the literature on African diasporan philanthropy in the Americas focuses on African American practices in the United States. Carson's seminal work (1993) demonstrates the integral role of the black church as an all-purpose philanthropic and social service institution for African Americans from the colonial through contemporary period. In many ways, black churches can be seen as the forebears of contemporary community foundations in that they pooled members' funds for general community purposes. The underlying cultural principle of pooling individual funds for a community purpose may have been adapted from West Africa even though the formal institution of *esusu* does not seem to have existed in North America during the colonial period. Although the field would benefit from more historical research on this issue, the *esusu*-derived model of community philanthropy would have easily accommodated the standard financing structures of Western Christian denominations, for example, the Methodist church, on which some of the earliest African American churches were based. Thus, the traditional community philanthropy role of the black church may have be derived, at least in part, from the cultural principles, that is, grassroots pooling of resources for community use, from the West and Central African *esusu*.

African Americans also modified Western social institutions to accommodate African cultural principles of philanthropy. Some of the earliest Africanized American voluntary associations were Masonic secret societies. Although it is not clear that African American Masons operated rites-of-passage programs comparable to those indigenous to West Africa, the literature suggests that they clearly had features that may have been African in origin. For example, several scholars suggest that the ritual communication system used by African American Masons in the Prince Hall Masonic Lodge, created in 1755 and often cited as the first African American nonprofit organization, was at least in part African influenced (Siebert, 1898; Tobin and Dobard, 1999). Masons, along with other black self-help organizations, provided not only social outlets for members but practical assistance for others in the community, such as providing financial support or acting as agents in the Underground Railroad. Although the form of black Mason societies was European based, the content and function were very much rooted in African American tradition. Like the black church, black Masonic societies adapted a mainstream social institution to the culture and needs of America's black community. These early African American institutions, for example, secret societies as well as the church, can therefore be seen as a type of operating foundation since they pooled resources for the social good while also providing direct social services to members and the broader community. These and other early African American nonprofit organizations extended Africa's long-standing voluntary association traditions to the Americas (Harris, 1979).

The literature also suggests a clear tie between African and African Caribbean philanthropic practices since the colonial period. The African revolving community fund survived not only as a cultural principle but also as a distinctive social institution throughout the Caribbean. As recorded in colonial historical records, these funds often retained the names of their African predecessors. For example, historical records show that they are still called *esu* in the Bahamas; *susu* in Jamaica; and *esusu, susu,* or *sou sou* in Trinidad and Tobago, clearly reminiscent of the West African terms for this practice. Although there are minor differences in how these Caribbean variants operate, they all have the same general role as a community finance institution. Their existence is documented in both the colonial Caribbean and precolonial West and Central Africa, suggesting that they are not of European origin. Nor are they a more contemporary, conscious incorporation of West African cultural practices (Bascom, 1952). The African version of this worldwide practice survived the Middle Passage, in an adapted form, throughout black communities in the New World. It continues to function as a grassroots community finance tool throughout West and Central Africa and the Caribbean, with various mainstream nonprofit and government sector efforts to formalize and strengthen its role.

Contemporary African contributions to black philanthropy

Reflecting the diversity of Americans of African heritage, contemporary African diasporan philanthropy in America takes many forms. The immigration of growing numbers of Africans to the United States, particularly in the 1990s, also may have contributed to an emergent renaissance in black giving. There are a few studies that document African or U.S. African immigrant philanthropy and nonprofit sector activity. Relevant data are often embedded in sociological or political studies of African immigrant communities in the United States. There are a few case studies that specifically focus on issues of African immigrant nonprofit formation or philanthropy in particular cities. However, these are often in small journals with limited circulation. The available research does not permit conclusive generalizations about African giving practices in the United States. Thus, the trends suggested here are tentative and intended to promote discussion and further investigation.

Case study of African diasporan nonprofit formation in the Twin Cities of Minneapolis and St. Paul in Minnesota suggests that African philanthropy may focus mostly on direct social services to people from the same African community of origin. (According to the 2000 Census, the Twin Cities of Minnesota have the most diverse black population in the United States in terms of national origin.) Financial support to extended families in the United States and abroad may also be a key feature of African immigrant giving practices. In addition, there are panethnic, nationality-based mutual aid societies (for example, a Yoruba and an Igbo mutual aid society in Minnesota, as well as a Nigerian association) forming to influence both sociopolitical issues in Africa and strengthen panethnic identity in Minnesota (Copeland-Carson, 2003, 2004). These groups raise money mostly from members and receive in-kind support from diplomatic missions to support the needs in both America and their countries of origin. Associations tend to subsist primarily through in-kind support, membership dues, and occasionally special appropriations of public funds to support annual or one-time cultural events or related activities.

African and African Caribbean immigrants operate *esusu*-type revolving savings and loan pools for both individual and community purposes. African immigrants are also replicating in the United States philanthropic and other types of nonprofits originating from their homelands. For example, several Nigerian ethnic groups have recreated their traditional mutual aid associations in the Twin Cities and provide philanthropic as well as other support to members and the broader community. In addition, these organizations often support nonprofit causes in their country of origin. As exemplified by the prominent giving of sports stars, such as Akeem Olajuwon and Dikembe Mutombo, African immigrant philanthropy encompasses a spectrum of complexity, from the informal *esusu*-type to complex international private foundations (Aluoka, 2001).

The case study data also suggest that more informal civic associations are beginning to spawn formal nonprofits supported by African immigrant philanthropy as well as grants from foundations and the government and, perhaps to a lesser extent, fees for service. Although most of these nonprofits tend to focus on direct social service to people of the same national origin, for example, Ethiopians, the Minnesota case suggests that they are beginning to provide services to the broader public and engage in advocacy. As has been the general case with black people in the United States since the seventeenth century, religious institutions are a key forum for organizing philanthropic activity among contemporary immigrants as well. Funding, technical assistance, and social services from religious institutions (Muslim and Christian), both white and black American, have critical roles in supporting the emerging African immigrant nonprofit sector. These institutions are natural partners in philanthropy and nonprofit formation, as they are key agents in facilitating emigration of Africans from their countries of origin to the United States. In particular, African American churches with missionary activities in Africa or a pan-Africanist heritage, such as the African Methodist Episcopal church, may have a unique and continuing role in strengthening African diasporan philanthropy.

In addition, a recent trend is the creation of pan-African non-profit groups that include African Americans as well as Africans of various national origins to work on a variety of social programs in the local community and Africa. Traditional African American giving also continues to grow and flourish in Minnesota (Carson and Taylor, 1995). Given that, overall, blacks are still a small proportion of Minnesota's population and that the state has the most diverse black population in the United States, increasing pan-African efforts in the nonprofit sector may be a means to increase the scale and political influence of the state's black community (Copeland-Carson, 2004).

Conclusion: Toward a more inclusive black philanthropy

The changing demographics of America's African diaspora provides new opportunities to strengthen the impact of both African immigrant and African American philanthropy in the United States. This chapter suggests that we promote a notion of an African diaspora in the United States composed of diverse ethnic groupings (African American, Somali American, Haitian-American, Afro Cuban, and others). These diverse groups have different histories but may have mutual interests derived in part from their shared African ancestry and experience of racial discrimination or oppression in the Americas. This more expansive notion of identity can provide the conceptual foundation for a more inclusive black philanthropy that appreciates diasporan cultural diversity.

Translating an African diasporan perspective and research agenda on philanthropy into practical social action is a daunting challenge. While common racial affinity and, broadly, historical origins may be seen as a basis to begin cooperation between U.S.-born African Americans and African immigrant philanthropists, these factors are not sufficient for success. Sensitivity to intricate subcultural differences in gender relations, community organizing, verbal and non-verbal communication, as well as history and political issues among various African countries and ethnicities is also essential. Although there is always a place for culturally specific work based on the interests of one group, Africans, African Caribbeans, Afro Latins, and African Americans should try to make their respective non-profit boards and staffs more reflective of the diversity of America's African diaspora whenever feasible or possible.

African American culture has never been monolithic or static. It is part of a dynamic, diasporan complex of diverse cultural practices with distinctive regional and ethnic variations. The admixture of these multiple African cultures created the basis of a unique African American culture of which our philanthropic practices are one component. People of African heritage from throughout the world continue to add to the richness of Africans' cultural influence on America. Recapturing the roots of these giving traditions through inclusion of the contemporary diversity of all people of African descent in America can help revitalize and strengthen black philanthropy for all.

Note

1. These funds exist in many societies throughout the world. This chapter does not claim that revolving community funds originated in Africa. It suggests that the West and Central African revolving community fund type, as indicated by both linguistic and primary historical evidence, was adapted by African Caribbean and perhaps African American and Afro Latin persons in the New World and persists as a component of contemporary diasporan philanthropic traditions. It should be noted, however, that available primary historical evidence does not suggest that this form of revolving community fund existed among either Americans of European descent or European colonial powers in Africa (see Bascom, 1952). This suggests that the *esusu*-type funds in the Americas may have originated in West and Central Africa, where they apparently have been common for millennia.

References

Aluoka, O. "Diaspora Philanthropy: The Promise and Limitations in Strengthening Trans-Atlantic Giving by African and African Americans through Community Foundations." Graduate thesis, City University of New York, 2001.

Bascom, W. "The Esusu: A Yoruba Institution." *Journal of the Royal Anthropological Institute*, 1952, *82*(1), 63–69.

Boone, S. A. Radiance from the Water: Ideals of Feminine Beauty in Mende Art. New Haven, CT: Yale University Press, 1986.

Butt-Thompson, F. W. *West African Secret Societies: Their Organizations, Officials and Teachings*. New York: Argosy-Antiquarian, 1969. (Originally published in 1929.)

Carson, E. D. *A Hand Up: Black Philanthropy and Self-Help in America*. Washington, D.C.: Joint Center for Political and Economic Studies, 1993.

Carson, E. D., and Taylor, D. "Black Giving in Minnesota: The Tradition Continues." *Giving Forum*, Fall 1995, pp. 1–3.

Copeland-Carson, J. *Pan-African Philanthropy: Towards a New Conceptual Model of Black Giving*. Washington, D.C.: National Center for Black Philanthropy, 2003.

Copeland-Carson, J. *Creating Africa in America: Translocal Identity in an Emerging World City*. Philadelphia: University of Pennsylvania Press, 2004.

Feierman, S. "Reciprocity and Assistance in Precolonial Africa." In W. F. Ilchman, S. N. Katz, and E. L. Queen (eds.), *Philanthropy in the World's Traditions*. Indianapolis: Indiana University Press, 1998.

Harris, J. E. *Global Dimensions of the African Diaspora*. Washington, D.C.: Howard University Press, 1982.

Harris, R. L. "Early Black Benevolent Societies, 1780–1830." *Massachusetts Review*, 1979, *20*, 608–609.

Hine, D. C., and J. McLeod (eds.). *Crossing Boundaries: A Comparative History of Black People in the Diaspora*. Bloomington: Indiana University Press, 1999.

Holloway, J. E. (ed.). *Africanisms in American Culture*. Bloomington: Indiana University Press, 1990.

Iliffe, J. *The African Poor: A History*. Cambridge: Cambridge University Press, 1987.

Jalloh, A., and Maizlish, S. E. (eds.). *The African Diaspora*. Arlington: University of Texas, 1996.

Siebel, H. D. "Informal Finance: Origins, Evolutionary Trends and Donor Options." Paper presented at a conference on Advancing Microfinance in Rural West Africa, Bamako, Mali, Feb. 22–25, 2000.

Siebert, W. *The Underground Railroad: From Slavery to Freedom*. New York: Macmillan, 1898.

Thornton, J. K. *Africa and Africans in the Making of the Atlantic World, 1400–1800*. Cambridge: Cambridge University Press, 1992.

Tobin, J. D., and Dobard, R. G. *Hidden in Plain View: A Secret Story of Quilts and the Underground Railroad*. New York: Anchor Books, 1999.

Vickerman, M. *Crosscurrents: West Indian Immigrants and Race*. New York: Oxford University Press, 1999.

Walters, R. W. *Panafricanism in the African Diaspora*. Detroit: Wayne State University Press, 1993.

Yelvington, K. A. "The Anthropology of Afro-Latin America and the Caribbean." *Annual Review of Anthropology*, 2001, *30*, 227–260.

JACQUELINE COPELAND-CARSON *is director of U.S. Bancorp's Philanthropic Services Program and a senior fellow at the Humphrey Institute, University of Minnesota.*

Economic research about charitable giving among immigrant populations in the United States sheds light on charitable behaviors related to, but not often included in, discussions of black philanthropy.

9

Immigrant assimilation and charitable giving

Una Okonkwo Osili, Dan Du

IT IS OFTEN ARGUED that successful integration of new immigrants into host societies is important for economic progress and social cohesion. One indicator that can shed new light on the complex process of immigrant assimilation is charitable giving. Charitable giving and other forms of civic engagement have been shown to affect norms of trust, connectedness, and the ability of individuals and communities to enhance their economic and social well-being through cooperative behavior (Putnam, 1993, 2000). By studying immigrant assimilation in charitable giving, it is possible to go beyond learning about immigrants' cultural values and norms and understand how they interact with America.

In this chapter, we examine immigrant assimilation in charitable giving. The results we present are related to broad questions concerning the economic and social dimensions of immigrant

We gratefully acknowledge funding from the Center on Philanthropy at Indiana University. We have benefited greatly from comments from Mark Wilhelm, Rich Steinberg, and participants at the 2003 ARNOVA conference. Xiaojun Feng and Jeanne Ruan provided excellent research assistance.

NEW DIRECTIONS FOR PHILANTHROPIC FUNDRAISING, NO. 48, SUMMER 2005 © WILEY PERIODICALS, INC.

assimilation. Our findings can also inform debates on the role that social identity and cultural origins play in shaping patterns of charitable giving and private transfer behavior.

Our empirical analysis is based on new data from the Center on Philanthropy Panel Study (COPPS), a module in the Panel Study of Income Dynamics (PSID). These data represent the largest one-time study of philanthropy in the United States and provide a unique opportunity to study the role of immigrant status on both charitable giving and private transfers.

We find that immigrant status has a negative but insignificant impact on charitable giving, and there is considerable evidence that immigrants adapt rapidly to U.S. charitable institutions. Our results on private transfers present a striking contrast. Private transfers generally refer to transfers of money and goods to individuals living outside the household. Immigrant households are about 10 percent more likely to participate in private transfer networks. However, these networks tend to be relatively persistent as immigrants gain U.S. experience. Our results on charitable giving, and to a lesser extent private transfer networks, provide some evidence that immigrants assimilate to American processes and institutions and perhaps may have the potential to shape social and civic life in the future.

Background

Despite the lack of quantitative sources on patterns of giving among U.S. immigrants, there is a growing body of descriptive literature that examines how ethnicity and cultural traditions affect giving patterns. Recent immigrants often arrive in the United States with their own traditions of giving based on experiences in their country of origin, which may differ from giving traditions of the native-born population (Joseph, 1995).[1] Furthermore, recent immigrants may have lower levels of involvement with U.S. charitable institutions due to residential segregation and social networks.

There is also some evidence that private transfers are common among immigrant households (O'Neill and Roberts, 2000). Although there is likely to be a great deal of heterogeneity within immigrant populations, the contribution of time, goods, and money in less formal and more personal ways has been an important part of the U.S. immigration experience. Private transfers within extended family and social networks often include financial support toward education expenses, medical costs, and housing, and improve the ability of nonhousehold recipients to cope with adverse shocks to income, including those associated with unemployment and ill health (Chao, 1999). Migrants' family ties and social networks outside the United States may also affect patterns of private transfer behavior. Immigrants with immediate family members residing outside the United States may send remittances to family members or channel their resource transfers toward home town organizations and community development projects.[2]

An extensive literature documents the importance of private transfer networks in developing countries, where a growing share of U.S. immigrants originates (see Morduch, 1999, for a detailed review of this literature). Private transfers may be motivated by the altruistic ties and reciprocity norms that link family members and close friends, as well as by exchange considerations. To understand transfer patterns among immigrants, Chao (1999) argues that immigrants may not often recognize informal giving as philanthropy, but rather may consider this to be part of an individual's social obligation to family and social networks.

Our focus on immigrant assimilation in charitable giving fits into a broader literature on the economic and social adaptation of U.S. immigrants. Although the assimilation of immigrants in philanthropic activity is a relatively unexplored topic, there may be some parallels with the wage assimilation literature.[3] In particular, levels and composition of formal and informal giving among U.S. immigrants may converge to that of the native-born population. It is likely that the rate of assimilation in charitable giving will depend on the immigrant's country-of-origin experience. Specifically, the degree of similarity between philanthropic institutions in the country of origin and the host country may affect the rate of assimilation in charitable giving. Immigrants from ethnic traditions and countries with less similar philanthropic institutions (compared to the United States) may assimilate at a slower rate compared with immigrants from countries with more similar philanthropic institutions, other things being equal.

There is also some evidence that assimilation among new immigrants, which is mainly composed of Latin American and Asian immigrants, may occur at a slower rate when compared to the pace of assimilation achieved by earlier waves of European immigrants (Borjas, 1994).[4] There is likely to be a great deal of heterogeneity based on ethnicity and country of origin (Duleep and Regents, 1997), as some national origin groups appear to experience faster economic assimilation than others.

Results

We first present results from our baseline model, which includes the indicator variable for immigrant status.

Charitable giving

From Table 9.1, column 1, we note that immigrant status does not have a statistically significant impact on the probability of giving and the level of charitable giving, after we have introduced controls for permanent income and other household variables. We augment our basic specification in order to study immigrant assimilation in charitable giving. In column 2, we adopt a flexible specification to examine the impact of immigrants' duration of stay in the United States on charitable giving. Interestingly, we find that only recent immigrants (who migrated in the past ten years to the United States) have a significantly lower likelihood of giving (the omitted category is immigrants with more than thirty years of U.S. experience). Our results suggest that there are assimilation effects in charitable giving.[5] In particular, as immigrants gain U.S. experience, their participation and levels of charitable giving appear to converge to native patterns.[6]

Private transfers

From Table 9.1, column 1 in the bottom panel, starting at the mean, we find that immigrants are 11 percent more likely to give private transfers. The levels of private transfers (measured in logs) are also significantly higher among immigrant households. Conditional on giving, we find that the level of private transfers is about 83.4 percent higher for immigrant households. Unlike our results on charitable giving, immigrants appear more likely to engage in private transfer networks even after we have controlled for economic and demographic variables.

Column 2 in the bottom panel allows us to examine assimilation effects in private transfer behavior using a flexible specification for duration of stay. Our results indicate that immigrant participation in informal giving appears relatively persistent over time. Specifically, immigrants with ten to fifteen years of U.S. experience continue to have higher incidence and levels of private transfers, compared to the omitted category (immigrants with more than thirty years of U.S. experience). In contrast, our results for charitable giving suggest that only recent immigrants with less than ten years of U.S. experience are less likely to give to a charitable organization compared to the omitted category.

We also examine the interaction of immigrant status and years of U.S. experience (in years). Our results indicate that U.S. experience is associated with a decrease in the incidence, as well as the level of private transfers. In particular, an additional year in the United States reduces the likelihood that an immigrant will send a private transfer by about 0.5 percentage points. Again, these results present an interesting contrast to our results on formal charitable giving. While length of stay in the United States reduces immigrant participation in private transfer networks, it tends to increase immigrant participation in charitable giving.

Table 9.1. Probit and tobit regression results for charitable giving and private transfers

Dependent variable: Give to charitable institutions and level of charitable donation

	(1)				(2)				(3) Bivariate Probit and Tobit		
	Marginal Effect	Probit	Marginal Effect	Tobit	Marginal Effect	Probit	Marginal Effect	Tobit	Marginal Effect	Probit	Tobit
Immigrant	-0.02	-0.06 (0.09)	-0.23	-0.40 (0.27)	0.03	0.09 (0.26)	-0.11	-0.18 (0.90)	-0.01	-0.03 (0.09)	-0.32
Less than 10 years of stay					-0.24	-0.64* (0.33)	-0.90	-1.71 (1.10)			
10-15 years of stay					0.03	0.08 (0.30)	0.23	0.38 (1.00)			
15-30 years of stay					-0.03	-0.08 (0.27)	0.02	0.04 (0.93)			
Immigrant year*											
Number of observations		5,216		5,220		5,099		5,103		5,172	5,176
Log likelihood		-2,581		-10,976		-2,507		-10,700		-2,561	-13,901

Dependent variable: Give private transfer and level of private transfer

	(1)				(2)				(3) Bivariate Probit and Tobit		
	Marginal Effect	Probit	Marginal Effect	Tobit	Marginal Effect	Probit	Marginal Effect	Tobit	Marginal Effect	Probit	Tobit
Immigrant	0.11	0.50*** (0.10)	1.16	6.21*** (1.28)	-0.01	-0.09 (0.37)	-0.19	-1.15 (4.80)	0.10	0.50*** (0.10)	6.18*** (1.94)
Less than 10 years of stay					0.18	0.73* (0.42)	1.81	8.95* (5.36)			
10-15 years of stay					0.22	0.85** (0.40)	2.17	10.34** (5.10)			
15-30 years of stay					0.10	0.47 (0.38)	1.10	5.86 (4.90)			
Immigrant year*											
Number of observations		5,176		5,176		5,060		5,060		5,172	5,176
Log likelihood		-1,601		-3,124		-1,556		-3,023		-1,599	-13,901

Note: Contribution levels are measured as the natural logarithm plus 1. Robust standard errors are shown in parentheses. Our baseline model includes immigrant, the natural logarithm of giving price, linear, quadratic age terms, male, married, years of education, unemployed, nonwhite, Catholic, family size, and natural logarithm of permanent family income and regional dummies. Regional dummies include Northeast, Southeast, North Central, South Central, Mountain and West of U.S. states. Default: foreign countries.

*Significant at 0.1 level. **Significant at 0.05 level. ***Significant at 0.01 level.

Household variables

We now turn to a discussion of other variables related to immigrant charitable giving: giving to religious, nonreligious, and international giving of immigrants; the impact of immigrants' region of origin on the incidence of charitable giving and private transfers; and the underlying causes of the immigrant-native gaps in participation in charitable giving and private transfers.

Organization-specific results. Table 9.2 allows us to investigate immigrant-native differences in specific types of charitable institutions. We examine giving to religious, nonreligious institutions, and international giving. The key dependent variables are defined as (1) whether an individual contributed formally to this specific category in the survey period and (2) the log total amount contributed in the survey period (not available for international giving).

In specification 1, we report only the coefficients on immigrant status without controls for duration of stay in the United States. From Table 9.2 (specification 1), immigrant status has a negative but insignificant impact on the incidence and levels of religious giving. Interestingly, immigrants appear significantly less likely to give to nonreligious institutions, and their levels of giving are lower. The notable exception here is international giving, where we find that immigrants are actually 4 percentage points more likely to give to international charitable activities, holding other variables constant.

Specification 2 includes controls for duration of stay. Consistent with earlier results, U.S. experience has a positive effect on charitable giving to religious institutions. In addition, we find that immigrant status no longer has a statistically significant impact on nonreligious giving once we control for immigrants' duration of stay.[7]

Region of origin. In Table 9.3, we examine the effect of immigrants' region of origin on the incidence of charitable giving and private transfers. Our results include controls for duration of stay.

From Table 9.3, immigrants from the Middle East, Africa, and South America are less likely to participate in charitable giving compared to the excluded category (European immigrants), although these results are not statistically significant. However, we

Table 9.2. Organization-specific results: Giving to religious, nonreligious, and international purposes

Dependent variable: Give to charitable institution and level of charitable donations

	(1) Religious				(2) Nonreligious				(3) International	
	Marginal Effect	Probit	Marginal Effect	Tobit	Marginal Effect	Probit	Marginal Effect	Tobit	Marginal Effect	Probit
Specification 1: No duration-of-stay controls										
Immigrant	-0.004	-0.01 (0.09)	-0.05	-0.14 (0.44)	-0.12	-0.30*** (0.09)	-0.53	1.29*** (0.32)	0.04	0.61*** (0.18)
Number of observations		5,218		5,141		5,202		5,077		5,219
Log likelihood		-3,155		-9,061		-2,870		-9,207		-524
Specification 2: With duration-of-stay controls										
Immigrant	-0.08	-0.20 (0.26)	-0.44	-1.28 (1.47)	-0.01	-0.04 (0.25)	-0.08	-0.18 (1.07)		
Less than 10 years of stay	-0.05	-0.14 (0.33)	-0.23	-0.66 (1.80)	-0.20	-0.50 (0.32)	-0.78	-1.99 (1.32)		
10-15 years of stay	0.16	0.40 (0.30)	0.86	2.10 (1.63)	-0.11	-0.29 (0.30)	-0.50	-1.21 (1.21)		
15-30 years of stay	0.10	0.25 (0.27)	0.63	1.58 (1.52)	-0.09	-0.21 (0.27)	-0.37	-0.88 (1.12)		
Number of observations		5,101		5,026		5,086		4,962		
Log likelihood		-3,090		-8,930		-2,817		-9,096		

Note: Contribution levels are measured as the natural logarithm plus 1. Robust standard errors are shown in parentheses. Our baseline model includes immigrant, the natural logarithm of giving price, linear, quadratic age terms, male, married, years of education, unemployed, nonwhite, Catholic, family size, and natural logarithm of permanent family income and regional dummies. Regional dummies include Northeast, Southeast, North Central, South Central, Mountain and West of U.S. states. Default: foreign countries.

*Significant at 0.1 level. **Significant at 0.05 level. ***Significant at 0.01 level.

find that immigrants from Central America and Mexico are significantly more likely to participate in charitable giving than the omitted category (European immigrants). These results may provide some preliminary evidence that ethnicity and national origin influence the incidence of charitable giving, even after we have controlled for income and demographic variables. Immigrants from ethnic traditions and countries with less similar philanthropic institutions (to the United States) may have lower participation rates in formal philanthropy compared to immigrants from countries with more similar philanthropic institutions, other things being equal.

Table 9.3 also uncovers interesting results on private transfer behavior among immigrant households. From column 2, immi-

Table 9.3. Charitable giving and private transfers: Region of Origin

Dependent variable: Give to charitable institution controls for duration of stay

Default: Europe			*(Full Sample)*	
	Charitable Giving		*Private Transfers*	
	Marginal Effect	*Probit*	*Marginal Effect*	*Probit*
Middle East and Africa	−0.06	−0.19	0.07	0.36
		(0.46)		(0.51)
Asia	0.02	0.08	0.05	0.28
		(0.34)		(0.38)
Central America and Mexico	0.15	0.56*	0.07	0.36
		(0.30)		(0.35)
South America	−0.21	−0.57	−0.03	−0.21
		(0.50)		(0.63)
Caribbean	0.03	0.08	0.22	0.84*
		(0.46)		(0.47)
Number of observations		4,520		4,484
Log likelihood		−2,195		−1,385

Note: Robust standard errors are shown in parentheses. Our baseline model includes immigrant, the natural logarithm of giving price, linear, quadratic age terms, male, married, years of education, unemployed, nonwhite, Catholic, family size, and natural logarithm of permanent family income and regional dummies. Regional dummies include Northeast, Southeast, North Central, South Central, Mountain and West of U.S. states. Default: foreign countries.

*Significant at 0.1 level.

grants from the Middle East and Africa, Central America and Mexico, and the Caribbean are more likely to participate in private transfer networks. However, only Caribbean immigrants are significantly more likely to participate in private transfer networks than the excluded category (European immigrants). Again, these results are suggestive of the role of home country experience in shaping both patterns of charitable giving and private transfer behavior.

Decomposing the immigrant-native gap in formal and informal giving. In this section, our goal is to investigate possible causes of the immigrant-native gaps in participation in charitable giving and private transfers. Specifically, we quantify the share of the immigrant-native gap that can be attributed to measurable characteristics (such as income, age, education, price of giving, and race) and the share that is due to structural or unobserved differences across immigrants and natives. Given the nonlinearity of the probit equation, we adopt a variation of the Blinder-Oaxaca decomposition (Blinder, 1973; Oaxaca, 1973). This method is detailed in Fairlie (2003).

Table 9.4 presents estimates using these methods for the nonlinear decomposition of the immigrant-native gap in charitable giving and private transfer behavior based on Fairlie (2003). Estimates presented in specifications 1 and 2 are based on the coefficients from the probit model for the immigrant and native samples, respectively.

We first discuss results from charitable giving. Although the selection of native or immigrant weights is somewhat arbitrary, it can be argued that from a policy viewpoint, it would be most useful to consider what would happen to immigrant participation in charitable giving if immigrants retained their own functions but were given the native means. From our estimates, about 59 percent of the immigrant-native gap would remain even if immigrants had the same income, education, and other measured characteristics as natives. When native coefficients are used (specification 2), a different picture emerges in that over 90 percent of the gap in formal giving can be explained by immigrant-native differences in characteristics.

Table 9.4. Decomposition of difference between native and immigrant in charitable giving and private transfer

	Charitable Giving		Private Transfers	
	Immigrant	Native	Immigrant	Native
Full Sample				
Mean:	0.451	0.681	0.173	0.095
Gap:		0.230		−0.078
	(1)	(2)	(3)	(4)
Overall difference:				
From ($X^N - X^I$)	0.09	0.23	0.038	0.022
	40.51%	98.05%	−48.37%	−28.59%
From ($\beta^N - \beta^I$)	0.14	0.004	−0.115	−0.100
	59.39%	1.86%	148.03%	128.24%
Random Sample				
Contribution to the gap from the following variables:				
Log permanent family income	0.050	0.048	0.040	0.015
	21.85%	21.00%	−51.76%	−18.79%
Education	0.062	0.088	−0.004	0.004
	26.76%	38.46%	4.90%	−5.33%
Nonwhite	−0.059	0.028	0.030	−0.022
	−25.59%	12.04%	39.07%	28.12%
Log price	0.034	0.027	0.009	−0.002
	14.96%	11.66%	−12.17%	3.17%
All other variables	0.010	0.016	0.018	0.021
	4.40%	7.13%	−23.30%	−26.36%

Note: Column 1 uses the coefficients from PROBIT with the immigrant sample. Column 2 uses the coefficients from PROBIT with the native sample.

We now turn to examine the contribution of individual characteristics to the overall gap in formal giving. Of particular interest is the relative contribution of group differences in racial background, income, and educational attainment to the immigrant-native gap in charitable giving. As expected, group differences in educational attainment and income account for a large share of the immigrant-native gap. Specifically, lower levels of educational attainment for immigrants account for 26 to 38 percent of the immigrant-native gap in charitable giving. Similarly, lower levels of income among immigrants account for about 21 percent of the immigrant-native gap in charitable giving, and this result appears less sensitive to the specification adopted. We note that our results suggest that group differences in age, marital status, and household size explain a relatively small share of the gap in charitable giving.[8]

In Table 9.4, we also present the decomposition results for private transfers. Specification 1 presents estimates based on immigrant coefficients, and specification 2 is based on native coefficients. In both specifications, the bulk of the immigrant-native gap in private transfers is attributable to differences in the coefficients rather than group differences in characteristics.

From our decomposition estimates, immigrant-native differences in charitable giving may be due to the distribution of individual characteristics (education, income, wealth, price of giving, demographic variables), as well as to the immigrant-native differences in the processes that generate formal giving. In contrast, much of the gap in private transfer behavior cannot be attributed to immigrant-native differences in characteristics. Instead, immigrant-native differences in private transfer behavior appear to be better explained by the differences in the processes that generate private transfers and omitted variables in our analysis, such as extended family characteristics and networks.[9] An important concern with the decomposition methodology is that we cannot address the concern that observed differences in characteristics for immigrants and natives (such as income, employment status, and education) may themselves be due to factors such as discrimination or social networks (such as language proficiency, home country ties, social networks, and residential segregation).

***

Conclusion

There has been a growing interest on the impact of immigration on social cohesion and institutions in the United States. Standard economic indicators provide only limited insights on how immigration will affect social and economic institutions, norms, and processes. This chapter provides new evidence on immigrant participation and assimilation in charitable giving in the United States.

Charitable giving is thought to be an intrinsic aspect of American life and may reflect norms of trust, connectedness, and cooperative behavior.

We find that while immigrant households appear to have lower average rates of participation and levels of charitable giving, these differences are not statistically significant after we have controlled for permanent income and other household variables. In contrast, immigrants are significantly more likely to give within private transfer networks compared to native households, holding other variables constant. From our results, immigrants tend to adapt relatively quickly to U.S. philanthropic institutions. We find that only recent immigrants (who arrived in the 1990s) have significantly lower rates of charitable giving.

Our results suggest that immigrant assimilation in charitable giving occurs rapidly, with implications for building social cohesion at the community and national levels. We also find that private transfer behavior is relatively persistent over time, suggesting that immigrants may have the potential to shape charitable giving and other U.S. social and economic processes over time.

Notes

1. An important source within this literature is *Donors of Color* (Council of Foundations, 1993), which uses qualitative methods to study traditions of giving within specific ethnic and cultural groups.

2. In 2001, remittances to developing countries amounted to $72.3 billion, exceeding total official flows, and nearly 42 percent of total foreign direct investment to developing countries (World Bank, 2003). In addition to financial transfers, immigrants may send clothing, food, and consumer goods to their family members in their origin communities. This figure represents a lower bound for the scale of remittances since remittance flows may also occur through informal channels.

3. Some studies of immigrant earnings, for example, Chiswick (1978), present a favorable picture of immigrant adaptation to the U.S. labor market. First, the earnings of immigrants grow rapidly as they gain experience in the United States; second, this rapid growth leads to immigrants' earnings outpacing the earnings of the natives within ten to fifteen years.

4. Borjas (1985) argues that the use of cross-sectional data may overstate the rate of wage assimilation.

5. We should note that there are some limitations because we rely on cross-sectional data on charitable giving. Ideally, longitudinal data would allow us

to observe a given household over time, enabling us to separately identify the role of cohort or time-of-arrival effects and duration effects in the assimilation process.

6. We also examine the inclusion of the immigrant's length of stay (in years) in the United States and its interaction with immigrant status (results not shown). The parameter on the duration-of-stay variable captures how an additional year in the United States affects the immigrant's likelihood of giving. From our results, an additional year in the United States has a positive effect on charitable giving.

7. We also examine more detailed information on the impact of immigrant status on giving for eleven categories of formal charitable activity. We find that immigrant status has a negative and statistically significant impact only on the incidence of charitable giving to the needy and educational and arts institutions, not on other categories of charitable giving.

8. From the decomposition results presented, estimates appear sensitive to whether native or immigrant coefficients are used. This is expected since the underlying processes that determine formal giving may differ across immigrant and native households. A likelihood ratio test rejects the null hypothesis that the coefficients for both specifications are identical.

9. We include the number of parents and siblings residing outside the United States in our estimation, but this does not significantly affect our baseline regression model. An additional parent or sibling residing outside the United States has a positive but insignificant effect on both charitable giving and private transfers.

References

Blinder, A. S. "Wage Discrimination: Reduced Form and Structural Estimates." *Journal of Human Resources*, 1973, *8*(4), 436–455.

Borjas, G. J. "Assimilation, Changes in Cohort Quality, and the Earnings of Immigrants." *Journal of Labor Economics*, 1985, *3*(4), 463–489.

Borjas, G. J. "The Economics of Immigration." *Journal of Economic Literature*, 1994, *32*(4), 1667–1717.

Chao, J. "Asian-American Philanthropy: Expanding Circles of Participation." 1999. [http://www.cof.org/culturescaring/AsianAmerican.pdf].

Chiswick, B. R. "The Effect of Americanization on the Earnings of Foreign-Born Men." *Journal of Political Economy*, 1978, *86*(5), 897–921.

Council on Foundations and Association of Black Foundation Executives. *Donors of Color: A New Promising Frontier for Community Foundations.* Washington, D.C.: Council on Foundations and Association of Black Foundation Executives, 1993.

Duleep, H. O., and Regents, M. R. "Immigrant Entry Earnings and Human Capital Growth: Evidence from the 1960–1980 Censuses." *Research in Labor Economics*, 1997, *16*, 297–317.

Fairlie, R. W. "An Extension of the Blinder-Oaxaca Decomposition Technique to Logit and Probit Models." Discussion paper 873, Economic Growth Center, Yale University, 2003.

Joseph, J. A. *Remaking America: How Benevolent Traditions of Many Cultures Are Transforming Our National Life.* San Francisco: Jossey-Bass, 1995.

Morduch, J. "Between the State and the Market: Can Informal Insurance Patch the Safety Net?" *World Bank Research Observer,* 1999, *14*(2), 187–207.

Oaxaca, R. "Male-Female Wage Differentials in Urban Labor Markets." *International Economic Review,* 1973, *14,* 673–709.

O'Neill, M., and Roberts, W. L. *Giving and Volunteering in California.* San Francisco: Institute for Nonprofit Organization Management, College of Professional Studies, University of San Francisco, 2000.

Putnam, R. *Making Democracy Work: Civic Traditions in Modern Italy.* Princeton, N.J.: Princeton University Press, 1993.

Putnam, R. *Bowling Alone: The Collapse and Revival of American Community.* New York: Simon & Schuster, 2000.

World Bank. *Global Development Finance.* Washington, D.C.: World Bank, 2003.

UNA OKONKWO OSILI *is assistant professor of economics at Indiana University–Purdue University Indianapolis.*

DAN DU *recently completed a master's degree in economics at Indiana University–Purdue University Indianapolis.*

A scholar provides a firsthand account of his introduction to the history and sociology of race philanthropy.

10

Race philanthropy: Personalities, institutions, networks, and communities

John H. Stanfield

THIRTY YEARS AGO when I entered Northwestern University as a doctoral student in sociology, there was no such thing as a field called philanthropic studies. Certainly there were scholars who wrote on the lives and work of those with surplus capital and human resources who gave their time, their money, and other resources to advance what they defined as a public good. But philanthropic studies as a multidisciplinary and interdisciplinary field with professional associations, academic and practitioner journals, and university-based and independent centers of research, policy, and practice support did not begin to appear until the 1980s.

As a subfield of philanthropic studies, race philanthropy is, like its disciplinary parent, a recent endeavor. Although for years scholars have written about the roles of foundations in black life, civic participation in black communities, and traditions of charity and volunteerism in black communities and populations, it was only in the 1980s that we began to develop a literature on race philanthropy in the social sciences and humanities. And it is even more

NEW DIRECTIONS FOR PHILANTHROPIC FUNDRAISING, NO. 48, SUMMER 2005 © WILEY PERIODICALS, INC.

recently that we have observed scholars writing about race philanthropy involving other nonblack people of color.

My sojourn as a student of race philanthropy, with the focus on the historical organizational contexts of the lives of philanthropists and foundation administrators who sponsored the careers, institutions, and movements of those social scientists and social commentators who interpreted the changing status of blacks and transformations in white-black relations in the last decades of legal Jim Crow, began at Northwestern. In the early 1970s, besides an unusual openness for creative cross-discipline research, there was something in the air in the Northwestern University Sociology Department that would establish a cohort of now senior black sociologists in major research universities who would make their name by doing original work demonstrating the empirical importance of historical materialism in analyzing institutions, communities, movements, and societies. Historical materialism was a central concept we all learned from the same classical theory professor, Arnold Feldman, or from his star student, Jim Pitts, a brilliant young African American sociologist who was also on the faculty. What Feldman instilled in us along with Pitts is that it is important not to reify by attributing institutional policies and practices to impersonal forces such as dynamics. Instead, it is critical to understand that institutions, communities, movements, and societies are human collectivities designed, managed, and transformed by real people, doing real concrete things like making decisions in the seats of organizational power. These powerful people as human beings have life histories, values, preferences, prejudices, and other human characteristics. Men and women run institutions, communities, movements, societies, and, for that matter, world systems with intentional attitudes, beliefs, and consciousness or with taken-for-granted attitudes and beliefs. They are socialized into their seats of institutional power and, before then, in their family and community contexts and in their informal networks of friends, peers, and social status circles.

If the records and access are available, the humanity of such powerful individuals and their organizational contexts can be reconstructed through the use of archival and other organizational and personal records, oral histories and other interview techniques, and even ethnographic work. This was an unusual way to train black sociologists (in fact, all sociologists), since what it means is that we were encouraged to study powerful whites in their institutional and broader societal locations rather than the usual way sociologists are professionalized: to look at the other end, the receiving end of power relations, that is, the impact and other outcomes of policies on populations rather than on the policymakers in their various life and career contexts.

For instance, John Sibley Butler, now a distinguished professor of sociology and business at the University of Texas Austin, did the first sociological study of the army in his dissertation, which demonstrated that the army did indeed practice institutional racism, and he demonstrated how those in power did so. Another example is Charles Payne, now a distinguished professor at Duke University, who did his dissertation and first book on the role of decision makers in inner-city schools in producing black youth who became academic failures. And then there was my work on philanthropic foundations and the so-called Negro problem in social sciences and in society in general between the two world wars, a time of dramatic status changes for whites and blacks in the last decades of Jim Crow as a national policy and dominant segregative thought pattern.

I stumbled on my topic quite inadvertently. I went to graduate school planning to become a sociologist of knowledge and found myself, in my first term, reading a string of classical sociological texts on race relations, which meant on blacks, since until very recently, the sociological study of race relations was synonymous with the study of black folks. By the early 1970s, the book-length studies we read (published in the 1930s) were long forgotten in main street sociology: Charles S. Johnson's *Shadow of the Plantation*, E. Franklin Frazier's *The Negro Family in the United States*, Ira de A. Reid's *Negro Youth in a Minor Key*, Allison Davis's *Deep South*, John Dollard's *Caste and Class in a Southern Town*, and Arthur Raper's *Preface to Peasantry* are the titles I remember. I also remember being fascinated by not only the text of these studies but also their acknowledgments. What began to catch my eye were thanks extended to foundation funders. I wondered how these funders influenced the structures and the content of these authors' findings. In general, I began to think about the role of sponsorship in knowledge production. I even started to do a comparative study on the sponsorship of knowledge production about African Americans in literature and in social sciences for my dissertation but due to the unwieldy size of the project, I had to eliminate the literature comparison.

In the 1970s, there was still a widely held belief that science was a matter of logical inquiry and value freeness—that the scientific ideas circulated were the most logical or the most consistently validated through reliable methods, not that they were due to the politics of idea selection and the political battles that are so characteristic of scientific work. The notion that certain ideas, such as black pathology or black academic underachievement, were rooted in objective social science was very much part of the way in which sociologists viewed the history of research on black people. It was a radical thought that what became known about black people was the product of the life histories and values of the researchers. And what was exceedingly radical was the thought that the societal contextualized life histories, values, preferences, and prejudices of academic and financial sponsors of sociological and other social scientific research on blacks, and on race relations in general, had to be reconstructed if we were to understand the selection of and the domination of ideas about black people and the exclusion of other ideas.

All of this came home to me at Fisk University in Nashville, Tennessee, where I had traveled to examine the Charles S. Johnson Collection as part of my doctoral research. A day or two after my arrival, something happened that broadened my focus. It also demonstrated to me that in so many cases, what we decide to do as researchers is based on what we stumble across rather than on following the party line of our research design. On that day, while I was waiting for the special collections librarian to bring me another load of boxes from the Johnson papers, I noticed an archival collection box on the table that said Julius Rosenwald Fund Papers. I had, of course, heard of the Julius Rosenwald Fund, since that foundation had supported much of Johnson's research. But I had had no idea the Rosenwald Fund papers were at Fisk.

That was the beginning of my sustained fascination with race philanthropy issues as I dove into the collection of Rosenwald Fund papers. It is a rich collection of the professional correspondence of Edwin Embree, who was president of the fund between 1928 and 1948 and would become Charles S. Johnson's best friend as well as chief financial sponsor. For one chapter of my dissertation (1977), on philanthropy and the sponsorship of race relations sociology, I used correspondence and other documents in the Rosenwald Fund collection and in the Johnson papers to reconstruct the organizational context of the Rosenwald Fund and the roles of its president and trustee board in supporting a certain kind of race relations social science. I delved further into philanthropic sponsorship after completing my dissertation with the research for my first book, *Philanthropy and Jim Crow in American Social Science* (1985). It was during that early postdoctoral research that I received grants and fellowships to broaden the scope of my data collection in foundation archives such as Rockefeller, Carnegie, Ford, Phelps-Stokes, John Slater Fund, and the George Peabody Fund.

The more I probed, the more I realized the importance of using historical materials to do autobiographical and career development and social network analysis of the creation and transformations of a race philanthropic world that materialized after the end of the Civil War, prevailed mostly through the early 1940s, and then went into decline. It was a closely knit world, which dictated a great deal of race policy in this country during a time when the federal government had a hands-off policy concerning black people and major issues such as black education, civil rights, black health care, and race relations research. This world declined with the ushering in of federal intervention in the lives of blacks from the mid-1950s forward. Some of the more influential personalities in that world, who held so much sway in distributing money and providing behind-the-scenes political support for black causes in a segregated

America, have now been forgotten: Jackson Davis, who was the long-time white southern officer of the Rockefeller General Education Board between around 1910 and the early 1940s and as such was the major gatekeeper of funds for black segregated public and private education in the south and elsewhere. Davis was also Gunnar Myrdal's major guide and interpreter of the South for background research leading to the publication of his epic, *An American Dilemma* (1944). There was James Dillard of the Anne Jeanes Fund, whose name has been immortalized through Dillard University in New Orleans. He designed the renowned Jeanes Teachers Program, a long-term program to provide rotating teachers for rural black schools from the early 1900s through the mid-1950s. Another person of influence in the race philanthropy world was Will Alexander, vice president of the Rosenwald Fund and the executive director of the Commission on Interracial Cooperation, southern liberals' response to the National Association for the Advancement of Colored People (NAACP) but more conservative in approach, stressing improving segregated facilities for blacks throughout the South. John Hope, the president of Morehouse College and then of Atlanta University, became the designated black representative in the Rockefeller circles after the death of Booker T. Washington, their man on the spot in 1915. It would help that Hope was a classmate of John D. Rockefeller Jr. at Brown in the 1890s.

As the walls of Jim Crow began to tumble in the early 1950s, those race philanthropists and beneficiaries who were still living either transformed into integrationists, such as Edwin Embree, or became despondent or even right wing with the winds of change. Charles S. Johnson, some say, died of a broken heart in the late 1950s as it became apparent that many of his friends were, to his dismay, quite ambivalent about, if not resistant to, the 1954 *Brown v. Board of Education* decision and the civil rights movement as it emerged in the mid-1950s. One of his last essays, published in the *New York Times*, reflects that disappointment.

When I published *Philanthropy and Jim Crow in American Social Science*, I was still very much an Americanist, and the American focus of the text certainly demonstrates that narrow national inclination. Since that time, starting with a Fulbright Scholar appointment in Sierre Leone during the 1988–1989 academic year and a Social Science Research Council Advanced Foreign Affairs Fellow in Great Britain in 1990, I have become very much of an internationalist in my personal life and my research interests. I am writing a second edition of *Philanthropy and Jim Crow in American Social Science*. It will have a distinct international perspective. This is because between the 1890s and 1950s, American race philanthropy had some very important international linkages. American personalities such as Jackson Davis and Booker T. Washington not only greatly shaped race philanthropy in areas such as segregative black education in the United States but also in European colonies in Africa. There were race social scientists who crossed national and colonial boundaries during this period, who had their research funded by American foundations; these researchers have now been long forgotten, but they held great sway during their time.

This internationalization of American race philanthropy is not an original idea. It was first demonstrated in Kenneth King's *Pan-Africanism and Education*, published in 1971 and only briefly in print. It is a book that links the black American and the black African educational work of Phelps-Stokes Fund administrators in their life historical contexts. In my second edition, I plan to do the same by looking at the life, historical, and organizational contexts of philanthropists and their foundation officers and key personalities in other nongovernmental spheres, such as missionary societies, newspapers, and travelers who influenced thinking about blacks and other races through the lenses of amateur and professional social science research. But even with this work, the history and sociology of race philanthropy remain largely unexplored terrain and therefore worthy of much more comprehensive theory-driven study.

There is also a need for more comprehensive historical materialistic research into the role of foundations in the various phases of post–World War II America as this society has transformed from being a legally and traditionally segregated society to becoming a sporadically desegregating society to becoming a culturally pluralistic, multiracial society in which assimilation and integration are no longer viewed universally as being inevitable. During the multi-decade post–World War II period in which foundation giving is more greatly restrained by federal law, we nevertheless have yet to have comprehensive research studies. These must document how effective foundation founders and staff and their institutions and networks have been in midwifing or least tracking these transformations and what the foundation sector needs to do in the future: ensure that as the pluralization of this nation-state continues to become more complex and perplexing, we develop the societal policy strategies and citizen civic participation practices to be not only a multiracial society but also a multiracial democracy in reality rather than merely in terms of politically polite rhetorical claims.

References

King, K. *Pan-Africanism and Education*. New York: Oxford University Press, 1971.

Stanfield, J. H. II. "Race Rationalization as a Cohort Experience, 1928-1948." Unpublished doctoral dissertation, Northwestern University, 1977.

Stanfield, J. H. II. *Philanthropy and Jim Crow in American Social Science*. Westport, Conn.: Greenwood Press, 1985.

JOHN H. STANFIELD *is professor in the Department of African American and African Diaspora Studies, Indiana University Bloomington, and a nonresidential fellow at the William E. B. DuBois Institute, Harvard University.*

Metaphorical lessons in fundraising show fundraisers how to raise money in the black community.

11

Hopscotching in the neighborhood

Alice Green Burnette

I WANT TO WARN YOU about the pitfalls of "skipping steps" when trying to raise money in the black community. To "skip" has several meanings, including these:

- To proceed with alternating hops and steps in a nimble, light-hearted fashion
- To omit an interval, an item, or a step

When they set out into black neighborhoods, fundraisers—to their detriment—often tend to skip time-tested principles for successful fundraising. Forty years of experience have taught me that undisciplined skipping around, in search of donations in those neighborhoods, will not work.

The Nigerian Nobel laureate in literature, Wole Soyinka, reminds us, "Criticism, like charity, starts at home" (Gates, 2004). In that spirit, these comments are not directed to my white American colleagues, or my Asian, Hispanic, or Native American colleagues, or my African American colleagues. I am an equal opportunity critic of anyone who skips around in any neighborhood in a search for money.

Some cynics believe that skipping steps is okay when everybody is on the same page. You may remember a story about a group of

NEW DIRECTIONS FOR PHILANTHROPIC FUNDRAISING, NO. 48, SUMMER 2005 © WILEY PERIODICALS, INC.

old men who told the same jokes to each other for so long that they ended up giving each joke a number and all of them understood. ("One of the best ones I ever heard was Number 84.")

Following the orderly and disciplined rules of hopscotch may provide fundraisers with a better chance to succeed—and to win the game.

Hopscotch traces its roots to Britain during the early Roman Empire when it was used for military training exercises. To win, a player cannot step on a line and cannot skip a square because all squares must be navigated sequentially. The first player to complete the course successfully wins. Today, hopscotch is usually considered to be a "girls' game," and that is fine with me. It takes a lot of skill and dexterity in hopscotch—as it does in life—in order to win.

There are nine squares on my hopscotch course. The first square is a working knowledge of professional fundraising. Nothing can replace technical competence. It is a poor worker who blames his or her tools. Shame on the fundraiser who does not use our professional tools and then blames prospects for being unresponsive. Do not go into the neighborhood to raise money if you do not have a competent and mature understanding of our profession. In other words, do not go there if you do not know what you are doing.

To do your work, you must do the work—the research, the reading, the cultivation, the listening, the writing, and the stewardship. The day will surely come when you cannot delegate or postpone your work to avoid your responsibility to get it done. The day will also come when you will finally realize that your computer cannot do your work for you.

The second square on my hopscotch game is the understanding that our society is changing. By 2050, non-Hispanic whites will make up 50.1 percent of the population, a bare majority, compared to 69.4 percent in 2000. The black neighborhood will increase from 36 million in 2000 to 61 million in 2050 and will represent 14.6 percent of the total population (U.S. Bureau of the Census, cited in *New York Times*, 2004). These demographic shifts are rearranging our society, driving new types of choice making, and greatly altering historical power, social, and economic relationships.

Of course, corporate America is responding early and eagerly. It is no accident that the black neighborhood is being target-marketed as never before by companies promoting their vast array of products and services. And, as usual, the nonprofit sector is slow to catch on to these demographic shifts, but it eventually will because it must. The changes underway now are bringing new kinds of students, graduates, members, volunteers, and donors, and they all require new kinds of institutional direction and programmatic content.

Although we must remain mindful of the state of black America, as it existed in the past and as it exists today, we must resist the temptation to apply yesterday's solutions to today's challenges. Certainly there will be changes in the next five to ten years, and we may not be able to predict their exact nature. The challenge will be to remain cognizant of the contemporary condition and the inevitable changes in the neighborhood because we will need flexibility and wisdom to devise strategies appropriate for the future.

The third square refers to the strong new competition for the philanthropic dollar. The Internal Revenue Service grants tax-exempt status to eighty-three nonprofit groups every day (Strom, 2004). This new competition is particularly vigorous when the philanthropic dollar is sought in the black neighborhood. Although most majority institutions have been late in recognizing that black people are legitimate, and possibly significant, targets for financial donations, they are not too late.

Fundraisers raise more money when their appeals are progressive. This is the fourth square. In the black neighborhood, it used to be possible to obtain support on the basis of being needy and having simply survived. "We deserve support because we have not closed our doors" is a worn-out message that has limited appeal to donors who want to move forward, not backward.

Fifth, media outlets have focused so heavily on increased income in the black community that "black philanthropy" is becoming a frequently used descriptor of our financial capacity. In fact—and somewhat ironically—the public perception of black philanthropy may be nurturing the tendency of fundraisers to "skip around" in the neighborhood.

According to the Selig Center for Economic Growth at the University of Georgia (2004), the buying power of African Americans would be $723 billion in 2004, a sum that would make our neighborhood rank as the ninth richest country in the world. However, fundraisers who seek success in this neighborhood must keep those billions in perspective by recognizing that many African Americans remain in a social and economic morass that should be unacceptable:

• In 2002, one of every four black men in the United States was unemployed—completely idle, jobless, and a nonparticipant in the economy (Herbert, 2004).

• In 2003, the percentage of African Americans age twenty-five or older who had a bachelor's degree or higher was a mere 17.3 percent ("USA Today Snapshots," 2004). Compare this to 11.4 percent of Hispanics, 30 percent of non-Hispanic whites, and 49.8 percent of Asian Americans (U.S. Bureau of the Census, 2003).

• Banks deny mortgages and home improvement loans to blacks at twice the percentage that they deny such mortgages and loans to whites. At the current rate that the home ownership gap between whites and blacks is closing, it would take 1,664 years to close that gap (National Urban League, 2004; Muhammad, Davis, Lui, and Leondar-Wright, 2004).

• Health indicators in the black neighborhood are alarming: black people are more prone to sickness and die at disproportionate rates. Here are just three examples of the many health disparities in the neighborhood that we are struggling to overcome:

1. Infant mortality rates are more than twice as high among African Americans, even when socioeconomic conditions are considered (Institute of Medicine, 2002; Muhammad and others, 2004).

2. Mortality rates for African Americans and Native Americans with diabetes are more than twice that of white Americans (Institute of Medicine, 2002; Muhammad and others, 2004).

3. Black Americans make up slightly more than 12 percent of the population. In 2002, however, 42 percent of the 385,000 Americans living with AIDS were black Americans, and of the 40,000 newly diagnosed cases of HIV/AIDS, 54 percent were black. Researchers in North Carolina are studying the relationships between incarceration and the transmission of HIV/AIDS (Villarosa, 2004).

• On a broad scale, the matter of incarceration is a double-edged sword that debilitates the neighborhood. On one edge, up to 10 percent of the black male population under age forty is in jail, creating devastating effects on families, the neighborhood, and the nation. On the other edge, there are numerous statistics that few have acknowledged or addressed—for instance, in 2000, more than 80 percent of all drug users in the United States were not black people, but blacks represented nearly 50 percent of all drug possession arrests (Herbert, 2004; Jones, 2000).

• The gaps in both income and net worth persist. In 1968, African Americans had fifty-five cents for every dollar of white income. In 2001, we had fifty-seven cents. It took us thirty-three years to gain two cents. In 2001, the typical white household had a median household net worth of $121,000. The typical black household had a median household net worth of only $19,000, including home equity (Muhammad and others, 2004).

Why all the doom and gloom? There has been substantial progress in the neighborhood, and things are a lot better than they used to be, including in our philanthropic activities. A White House Council of Economic Advisors report (National Black United Fund, 2000) concluded that black Americans are more likely to give to charities than are whites. A detailed analysis in May 2003 in the *Chronicle of Philanthropy* (Anft and Lipman, 2003) compared average annual charitable giving by blacks and whites, relying on Bureau of Labor Statistics data; these were two of the findings:

- For people with incomes of $30,000 to $49,999, whites gave an annual average of $462 and blacks gave $528.
- For people with incomes of $50,000 or more, whites gave an annual average of $1,072 and blacks gave $1,204.

These data are encouraging. However, although blacks will put $723 billion into the U.S. economy in 2004, we—as a group and on a relative basis—still do not own very much, still do not produce very much, and still do not save very much. Every fundraiser should be honest about the true and total condition of the entire neighborhood and stop equating "increased income" with "increased wealth."

The sixth square is that the fundraiser who focuses on the needs and interests of prospects and donors will raise more money than the fundraiser who focuses primarily on the needs of his or her organization. Paul Schervish, director of the Center on Wealth and Philanthropy at Boston College, is my continuing education mentor in terms of this perspective. The needs and interests of people in the neighborhood may be different from what most fundraisers traditionally encounter. Therefore, all of us must bring much more depth and texture to relationship building in the black community. What does this mean?

"More depth and texture" means that history must be overcome. I do not mean history in some faraway, long-ago sense but rather history that has been endured as a life experience by most black prospects and donors. In their lifetimes, they were not welcome at colleges, universities, professional societies, museums, hospitals, and even churches. In the lifetimes of most black prospects and donors, exclusion was the norm and was mandated in many parts of our country.

"More depth and texture" means that although prospects may have discretionary resources to give, they also may be confronted with very real pressures that work against giving. The cold statistics of social and economic disparities in the neighborhood are translated into harsh realities of daily life for many, including those who have the capacity to give.

I suggest that the life of every adult African American has been touched by a close friend or family member who is in jail, who is pregnant but not married, who is sick with no health insurance, who has lost a job, who is on welfare, who is alcoholic or drug dependent, who is struggling to pay a child's tuition, and whose lifestyle is financed by indebtedness. These life-affecting problems pervade the neighborhood.

I acknowledge the fundraising successes of large and small black churches in the United States. They are much further along in terms of winning the hopscotch game, and fundraising professionals have a lot to learn from them. I also acknowledge the very few legitimately wealthy African Americans whose propensities to give are finally catching up with their capacities to give (Malveaux, 2004; Pogrebin, 2004). However, most prospects in the neighborhood need technical assistance and understanding from fundraisers before they will give their money away when their family members and friends are suffering. Fundraisers will not win if they simply skip through the neighborhood looking for some "black philanthropy money" rather than take the time to build relationships based on the true—and usually unspoken—needs of their prospects.

"More depth and texture" means that people in the neighborhood must learn to trust people they do not know as they plan and manage their money. We have felt ripped off and deceived by the whole range of financial institutions in our neighborhood.

We fundraisers have a tremendous amount of good work to do in the neighborhood. We all know that the coming transfer of wealth between generations will be the largest such event in history. Paul Schervish and his colleagues have estimated that this wealth transfer in the United States between 1998 and 2052 will be somewhere between $41 trillion and $136 trillion ("Doing Well and Doing Good," 2004).

An otherwise capable fundraiser asked me not too long ago, "Alice, what does that wealth transfer have to do with us?" Let me answer that question, as clearly as I can: all of us can either plan for the transfer of assets to the people and institutions we care about, or the government will decide, and all of us have the opportunity to be beneficiaries, as individuals or institutionally, of those transfers, or the government will decide. The most fundamental instrument needed to protect and transfer our assets as we want them to be handled is a will. Today, only 42 percent of American adults have a will, a significant drop from the 64 percent reported by the American Association for Retired People in 2000 (also see "Estate Confusion Results in Fewer Wills," 2004). In 2002, only 28 percent of the people in the black neighborhood had wills. This must change.

Imagine this if you are an African American with no will at the time of your death: your assets, including your share of those $723 billion that we control, will fly right out the window, maybe landing in places not to your liking. And you will wonder—as you watch from on high—why the greatest wealth transfer in history had no discernible effect on your children, your grandchildren, and all the institutions that you represent and care about.

The seventh square on my hopscotch board is a warning: do not be distracted or dazzled by the media. Keep your eye on the ball of what actually works in the neighborhood and not on what the media find interesting at the moment. Recall that Oseola McCarty's gift for student scholarships—$150,000 that she saved while working as a washerwoman of other peoples' clothes—received huge media attention. Contrast that with Alphonse Fletcher's gift of $50 million to stimulate progress fifty years after the *Brown* decision—$50 million he earned as a result of successful investment of other peoples' money—which received comparatively little media attention (Rimer, 2004). We need to celebrate all philanthropy and not only the giving that the media decide is important as a human interest matter.

This leads me to the eighth square: when we hopscotch in the neighborhood, we must provide proper stewardship of every gift. I do not really like the word *stewardship*. It sounds mechanical to me, consistent with the way that many fundraisers handle this essential step in our profession.

African American history is American history and, as a result, belongs to all Americans. Therefore, I can easily encourage all of you to remember this neighborhood history as you work to keep stewardship alive in your work. In 1766, Absalom Jones, a slave living in Philadelphia, married Mary King, who was also a slave. He eventually earned enough money to purchase her freedom. It took eight more years before he could purchase his own freedom in 1784. I consider that history to be an uncommon expression of stewardship—attending to the freedom of Mary King Jones first, before attending to his own.

Later, in 1787, Absalom Jones founded the Free African Society (considered by many as the birthplace of organized philanthropy in the neighborhood). This was almost seventy-five years before the Emancipation Proclamation that ended slavery in the United States and went into effect in 1863. Is your work really so difficult in comparison to that stewardship and neighborhood heritage?

The final, and ninth, square is this: in all things, be ethical. Decide early what your ethical standards will be. Be consistent. Be reliable. Be fair. Be faithful. Be truthful. Do what you say you will do. Our profession is becoming efficient and our execution is improving. However, efficiency without ethics will get you to the end of a game that you will not, cannot, and should not win.

In terms of the black experience, we have a rich tradition of sharing in the whole village, in the whole neighborhood. In terms of our philanthropy, we have followed the "Emmett Carson theorem": problem solving in the neighborhood always has been dynamic and responsive to making things better. Fundraising, not an easy business in most circumstances, is made more even difficult when fundraisers act like tourists in the neighborhood—just skipping through with limited understanding of and sensitivity to the local facts of life. We fundraisers cannot allow anyone to accuse us of having a "failure of imagination," to use a phrase coined by the 9/11 Commission.

The time-tested tools of our profession, the charitable impulse that already exists in the neighborhood, and our dedicated commitment to the achievement of a civil society can help us hopscotch in the neighborhood with confidence, purpose, productivity, and self-satisfaction.

References

American Association of Retired Persons. "Legal Documents." Washington, D.C.: American Association of Retired Persons, Apr. 2000.

Anft, M., and Lipman, H. "How Americans Give." *Chronicle of Philanthropy*, May 1, 2003.

Clemetson, L. "Links Between Prison and AIDS Affecting Blacks Inside and Out." *New York Times*, August 6, 2004, p. 1.

"Doing Well and Doing Good." *Economist*, July 31, 2004, pp. 57–59.

"Estate Confusion Results in Fewer Wills." Associated Press, June 7, 2004.

Gates, H. L., Jr. "When Democracy Is Not Enough: Criticism Begins at Home." *New York Times*, August 5, 2004, p. 23.

Herbert, B. "An Emerging Catastrophe." *New York Times*, July 19, 2004, p. 17.

Institute of Medicine. *Unequal Treatment: 2002*. Washington, D.C.: Institute of Medicine, 2002.

Jones, R. J. "The Truth About Black Crime." Jan. 16, 2000. [www.peace/ca/truthaboutblackcrime.com and www.hartford-hwp.com/archives/45a/193.html].

Malveaux, J. "The Real Deal on Black Unemployment." *Black Issues in Higher Education*, Aug. 12, 2004, p. 33.

Muhammad, D., Davis, A., Lui, M., and Leondar-Wright, B. *The State of the Dream 2004: Enduring Disparities in Black and White*. Boston: United for a Fair Economy, 2004.

National Black United Fund. "Opportunities and Challenges." Newark, N.J.: National Black United Fund, 2000.

National Urban League. *State of Black America 2004 Equality Index*. New York: National Urban League, 2004.

New York Times, Mar. 18, 2004.

Pogrebin, R. "Many Arts Groups Lag Behind in Black Trustees and Backing." *New York Times*, May 25, 2004, p. 1.

Rimer, S. "$50 Million Gift Aims to Further Legacy of *Brown* Case." *New York Times*, May 18, 2004, p. B2.

Selig Center for Economic Growth, University of Georgia. "The Multicultural Economy, 1990–2009." Athens: University of Georgia, Aug. 8, 2004. [http://www.selig.uga.edu/forecast/GBEC/GBEC032Q.pdf].

Strom, S. "Charitable Giving Holds Steady, Report Finds." *New York Times*, June 22, 2004, p. 12.

"USA Today Snapshots." *USA Today*, July 27, 2004, p. A1.

U.S. Bureau of the Census. *Report on Educational Attainment in the United States*. Washington, D.C.: U.S. Government Printing Office, 2003.

Villarosa, L. "Patients with H.I.V. Seen as Separated by a Racial Divide." *New York Times*, Aug. 7, 2004, p. 1.

ALICE GREEN BURNETTE *is principal of Advancement Solutions.*

Index

Back Issue/Subscription Order Form

Copy or detach and send to:

Jossey-Bass, A Wiley Company, 989 Market Street, San Francisco CA 94103-1741

Call or fax toll-free: Phone 888-378-2537 6:30AM – 3PM PST; Fax 888-481-2665

Back Issues: Please send me the following issues at $29 each
(Important: please include series initials and issue number, such as PF22.)

_____

_____

_____

$ _____   Total for single issues

$ _____   SHIPPING CHARGES: SURFACE   Domestic   Canadian

	First Item	$5.00	$6.00
	Each Add'l Item	$3.00	$1.50

For next-day and second-day delivery rates, call the number listed above.

Subscriptions: Please __start __renew my subscription to _New Directions for Philanthropic Fundraising_ for the year 2____ at the following rate:

U.S.	__Individual $109	__Institutional $228
Canada	__Individual $109	__Institutional $268
All Others	__Individual $133	__Institutional $302

**For more information about online subscriptions visit
www.interscience.wiley.com**

$ _____   Total single issues and subscriptions (Add appropriate sales tax for your state for single issue orders. No sales tax for U.S. subscriptions. Canadian residents, add GST for subscriptions and single issues.)

__Payment enclosed (U.S. check or money order only)

__VISA __MC __AmEx #_____ Exp. Date _____

Signature _____ Day Phone _____

__ Bill Me (U.S. institutional orders only. Purchase order required.)

Purchase order # _____
        Federal Tax ID13559302   **GST 89102 8052**

Name _____

Address _____

_____

Phone _____ E-mail _____

For more information about Jossey-Bass, visit our Web site at www.josseybass.com

Other Titles Available

NEW DIRECTIONS FOR PHILANTHROPIC FUNDRAISING